ARIAN

CHRISTIAN

BIBLE

Translation by: The Institute for Metaphysical Studies

Published by the Institute for Metaphysical Studies

This Bible is dedicated to,

Saint Arius of Alexandria

©2010 by the Institute for Metaphysical Studies
All rights reserved
Published by the Institute for Metaphysical Studies, USA
Printed in the USA
ISBN 1-4528-3955-7
EAN 978-1-4528-3955-4

Foreword

This work is in honor of the greatest, most influential thinker, philosopher and religious figure that the Western world has ever produced; this person is Jesus of Nazareth.

This work is based on the main premise of Arian[1] philosophy, and that is that Jesus of Nazareth was not God but a person.

The Arian view is that not only was Jesus of Nazareth not God, he was not even a god but a human being no different than any one of us ordinary people. He was a man, who, if his DNA could have been tested, it would have proved that he was the product of a man and a woman and that he shared the genes of this human mother and his human father.

Notwithstanding the desire of those who would will us to suspend our beliefs and common sense, there is nothing in the inventory of the shared experiences of everyday humans that suggests in any way that a person can rise from the dead, it just doesn't happen and it has never happened in a way that can be verified. Healing of the sick through 'spiritual means' is not uncommon and is something that we can accept from common experience. As far as raising the dead,

---

[1] See brief history of Arianism at the end of this Bible.

that is not what Jesus did, unless he lied. Whenever he raised someone from the dead, he said, probably in truth, that 'they were sleeping'.

The true history of what happened 2000 years ago will never be known except through faith, which is by definition, belief in something that cannot be proven or disproven.

The Divinity of Jesus of Nazareth is a very important matter to Christianity. Because if Jesus is not God, then what would be the need for those who claim to act as a conduit to God, i.e. the clergy. If Jesus were not part of the Trinity of God, then the connection between ordinary people, the church and God would be broken, to the detriment of the Church. At any rate, this did not happen. All of the monotheistic, political, major religions, Islam, Judaism, Catholicism and the Catholic based protestant sects that claim that Jesus is God, would rather fight than concede that their relationship with God is not eternal, natural and God-given. God as the supreme political leader of a religion or culture is quite seductive.

On the other hand, what are the arguments that support Jesus' humanity rather than his deity, other than the few reasons given above?

One thing is certain, that Jesus' view of God, or whatever motivated him was an internal matter. It was a private vision of things that we can never know. He described the kingdom of heaven as 'existing within our own hearts.', so if he identified with the kingdom of heaven as an internal reality, then that is probably where his experience of God, or what he called God, existed. (Probably based on the Judaic model described in the Hebrew scripture)

If Jesus was a God, then the things he accomplished was child's play for any God, raising the dead, healing the sick or arguing religious law with religious experts.

However, if Jesus was Just a man, then the things he did were marvelous, outstanding and worthy of respect and a product of great wisdom and wisdom such as the world has seldom, if ever, seen before.

For a God to give up his life when he knew he was going to be reborn and live in heaven just as if nothing had ever happened would have been nothing. For him to give up his life consciously of his own free will or to accept it as the will of God is amazing. No God could possibly do such a thing with the same level of sacrifice. As Jesus said, and I paraphrase, 'what matters is not the absolute amount that is given, but the relative amount that is sacrificed. That is to say that there is a difference in the quality of things that might be offered in sacrifice. The gift of a billionaire who gives a hundred million dollars is a much lesser gift tan the last dollar of a poor man, given to someone who is in desperate need of it.

It is the Arian contention that the only place the spirit of Jesus exist is in his words and in the hearts of people who read those words.

In the Holy Bible, there is a hierarchy of relevance, meaning and importance of the ideas presented. Of the two combined testaments, the Old Testament and the New Testament, the New Testament is superior because it contains the word of Jesus of Nazareth. The Old Testament is a religious history of the Jewish people that is a treasure trove of wisdom and cultural heritage. For any Christian, if there is a conflict between the two, then the New Testament and its new view of the world should win out. For instance, The Old Testament says that women who are adulterous and men who are homosexual should be stoned to death. On the other hand, Jesus in the Gospels of the New Testament tells us, "Do unto others as we would have them do unto us". The Old Testament says, "An eye for an eye and a tooth for a tooth", but Jesus said, "Turn the other cheek".

The Old Testament contains within itself the concept that men are meant to serve Scripture. Whereas,

Jesus, in the New Testament, in contrast, states quite clearly that, the scriptures are meant to serve men and not the other way around.

In the New Testament, there is another hierarchy of importance. Those Books of the New Testament that contain the words and sayings of Jesus are clearly more important that those Books that do not. Those Books, the Gospels of Mark, Luke and Matthew and John are the books that claim to report the actual words of Jesus. Christian scholars finalized the hierarchy, authenticity, veracity and authority of these by of these four Gospels by the order in which they were placed in the New Testament.

Matthew, Mark and Luke support one another in language, style and spirit and seem to have been written within the 'Jewish context' of Jesus and his disciples and the people to whom he ministered.

The Gospel of St John is different from the other three Gospels in tone and in the timing and nature of the events in Jesus' ministry. The Gospel of St. John also has anti-Semitic undertones that are a rebuke to Jesus' Jewish origins.

Therefore, the Gospel of John is not contained in the Arian Christian Bible. Those who wish to make their own comparison between John and the other Gospels can do so easily with any standard Bible. The Gospel of St John is like a stone among diamonds.

The main effort of this translation is to make the words of Jesus easier for the modern English speaker to understand, rather than to offer a different interpretation of Jesus' words other that the standard common interpretation of any other widely published Bible.

The Old Testament was combined with the New Testament as a contrast, not as an equal. To a Christian, in faith, practice and action, the teachings of Jesus as expressed by his words in the Gospels, is the superior source whenever there might be a conflict in meaning, and Christians should not be confused by this. The Old Testament is the Jewish Bible and it is use to conduct Jewish social, religious and cultural affairs.

The Arian Christian Bible is a presentation of the cream of the New Testament in the form of the words of Jesus of Nazareth as recorded in the three foremost Christian Gospels of Matthew, Mark and Luke.

The most apparent change in this Bible is the elimination of the use the 2nd per familiar case of the King James Old English translation. The pronouns thou, thee, thy and thine have been changed to 'you', 'your' and 'yours' and the case endings of 'st' and 'est' eliminated to reflect modern usage. i.e. (Goeth and goest). In some places the syntax of modern English is used where it does not affect commonly accepted sayings such as, Our Father who 'art' in heaven. In some places modern words are substituted for archaic forms such as, 'asked' or 'pleaded' instead of besought.

Jesus' words as related by his disciples are in bold type. Only those words that the disciples actually witnessed are presented here. Events that happened after Jesus' death are not covered in these gospels in accord with Arian teachings[2]. These events can be accessed from other biblical sources.

There are many translations of the Bible, some translate a word this way, and another translates a phrase that way. Ultimately, the only thing that matters is that sacred sense of what is right and what is not that resides in the heart of the reader.

Translated by,
The Institute for Metaphysical Studies
Charles D Levy, Director
director@metaphysicscenter.com

---

[2] See end section for discussion of Arian beliefs.

The Words of Jesus According to Matthew the Apostle

1. Jesus came from Galilee to Jordan seeking John, to be baptized by him. However, John forbade him, saying, I need to be baptized by you, and you come to me? Jesus answered saying, "**Suffer *it to be* now: for thus it becomes us to fulfill all righteousness.**" Then he allowed John to baptize him. Jesus, when he was baptized, went up straightway out of the water: and, lo, the heavens were opened unto him, and they saw the Spirit of God descending like a dove, and lighting upon him: And a voice from heaven came, saying, this is my beloved Son, in whom I am well pleased.
2. Then was Jesus led by the Spirit into the wilderness to be tempted of the devil. And after he had fasted forty days and forty nights, he was hungry. And when the tempter came to him, he said, 'If you are the Son of God, command that these stones be made bread.' However, he replied and said, "**It is written, man will not live by bread alone, but by every word that proceeds out of the mouth of God**".
3. Then the devil took him up into the holy city, and sat him on a pinnacle of the temple, and said to him, if you are the Son of God, cast yourself down. For it is written, He will give his angels charge concerning you: and in *their* hands they will bear you up, lest at any time you dash your foot against a stone.' Jesus responded, "**It is written again, you will not tempt the Lord your God**". Again, the devil took him up to an exceedingly high mountain, and showed him all the

kingdoms of the world and the glory of them; and said to him, 'All these things will I give you, if you will fall down and worships me.' At that, said Jesus to him, "**Get away, Satan: for it is written, you will worship the Lord your God, and him only will you serve."** Then the devil left him, and, behold, angels came and ministered to him.

4. Now when Jesus heard that John was cast into prison, he left for Galilee; And leaving Nazareth, he came and dwelt in Capernaum, which is upon the sea coast, in the borders of Zabulon and Nephthalim so that it might be fulfilled which was spoken by Esaias the prophet, who said. 'The land of Zabulon, and the land of Nephthalim, *by* the way of the sea, beyond Jordan, and Galilee of the Gentiles. The people who sat in darkness saw a great light; and to those who sat in the region of the shadow of death light sprung up about them.'

5. From that time, Jesus began to preach, and to say, "**Repent: for the kingdom of heaven is at hand."**

6. And Jesus, walking by the Sea of Galilee, saw two brothers; Simon called Peter, and Andrew his brother, casting a net into the sea, for they were fishermen. And he said to them, "**Follow me, and I will make you fishers of men**". And they straightway left *their* nets, and followed him. And going on from there, he saw other two brothers, James *the son* of Zebedee, and John his brother, in a ship with Zebedee their father, mending their nets; and he called them. And they immediately left the ship and their father, and followed him.

7. And Jesus went about all Galilee, teaching in their synagogues, and preaching the gospel of the kingdom, and healing all manner of sickness and all manner of disease

among the people. And his fame went throughout all Syria: and they brought to him all sick people who were taken with diverse diseases and torments, and those that were possessed by devils, and those who were lunatic, and those who had the palsy; and he healed them. And great multitudes of people followed him there, coming from as far as from Galilee, and from Decapolis, and from Jerusalem, and from Judaea, and from beyond Jordan.

8. Seeing the multitudes, he went up onto a mountain: and when he sat down, his disciples came to him: And he opened his mouth, and taught them, saying, **"Blessed *are* the poor in spirit: for theirs is the kingdom of heaven. Blessed *are* they that mourn: for they will be comforted. Blessed *are* the meek: for they will inherit the earth. Blessed *are* they who hunger and thirst after righteousness: for they will be filled. Blessed *are* the merciful: for they will obtain mercy. Blessed *are* the pure in heart: for they will see God. Blessed *are* the peacemakers: for they will be called the children of God. Blessed *are* they who are persecuted for righteousness sake: for theirs is the kingdom of heaven. Blessed are you, when *men* will revile you, and persecute *you,* and will say all manner of evil against you falsely, for my sake. Rejoice, and be exceedingly glad: for great *is* your reward in heaven: for in the same way they persecuted the prophets who came before you.**

9. **You are the salt of the earth: but if the salt has lost his savior, how can it be used to salt? It is thenceforth good for nothing, but to be cast out, and to be trodden under foot of men. You are the light of the world. A city that is**

set on a hill cannot be hidden. Nor do men light a candle, and put it under a bushel, but on a candlestick; and it gives light to all who are in the house. Let your light so shine before men, that they may see your good works, and glorify your Father who is in heaven.

10. Do not think that I am come to destroy the law, or the prophets: I have not come to destroy, but to fulfill. For verily, I say unto you, Till heaven and earth pass, not one jot or one title will in any way pass from the law, till all has been fulfilled. Whoever therefore will break one of these least commandments, and will teach men to do so, he will be called the least in the kingdom of heaven: but who ever will do and teach *them correctly,* the same will be called great in the kingdom of heaven. For I say to you, that unless your righteousness exceeds the righteousness of the scribes and Pharisees, you will in no case enter into the kingdom of heaven.

11. You have heard that it was said by them of olden times, 'That you shall not kill'; and who ever will kill will be in danger of the judgment of courts. But I say to you, That whoever is angry with his brother without a cause will be in danger of the supreme judgment: and whoever speaks to his brother with contempt will be in danger of the council: but whoever will say to his brother, 'You despicable fool', without reason, will be in danger of hell fire.

12. Therefore if you bring your gift to the altar, and remember that your brother has nothing against you; Leave your gift there before the altar, and go your way; Otherwise, first

try to reconcile with your brother, and then come and offer your gift.

13. Likewise, agree with your adversary quickly, while you are in the way with him; unless at some time, the adversary might deliver you to the judge, and the judge deliver you to the officer, so you can be cast into prison. Verily, I say to you, you will by no means come out from there until you have paid the last penny.

14. You have heard that it was said by them of olden times, 'You will not commit adultery': But I say to you, That whoever looks on a woman and lusts after her has committed adultery with her already in his heart. And if your right eye offends you, pluck it out, and cast *it* from you: for is it profitable for you that one of your members should perish, rather than allowing your whole body be cast into hell?

15. And if your right hand offends you, cut it off, and cast it from you. For it is profitable for you that one of your members should perish, rather than allowing your whole body to be cast into Hell?

16. It has been said, 'Whoever will put away his wife, let him give her a writing of divorcement:' But I say to you, That whoever divorces his wife, except for adultery, will cause her to commit adultery and whoever will marry her commits adultery also.

17. Again, you have heard that it has been said by them of olden times, 'You must not swear to do a thing and then not do it, but you should give your oaths to Jehovah, the Lord of oaths'. But I say to you, do not Swear at all; neither by heaven; for it is God's throne: Nor by the earth; for it is

his footstool: neither by Jerusalem; for it is the city of the great King. Neither will you swear by your head, because you cannot make one hair white or black. But let your communication be, yes, yes; no, no: for whatever is more than these comes from evil.

18. You have heard that it has been said, 'an eye for an eye, and a tooth for a tooth': But I say to you, that you should not resist evil. Whoever will hit you on your right cheek, turn to him the other cheek also. And if any man will sue you at the law, and take away your coat, let him have *your* cloak also. And who ever will compel you to go a mile, go with him two. Give to him who asks of you, and do not turn away from he who would borrow from you.

19. You have heard that it has been said; that you should love your neighbor, and hate your enemy. But I say to you, Love your enemies, and bless them that curse you. Do good to those who hate you, and pray for them who despitefully use you, and persecute you; So that you may be the children of your Father who is in heaven: for he makes his sun rise on the evil and on the good, and sends rain on the just and on the unjust. For, if you love only those who love you, what reward will you have? Do not even the publicans do the same? And if you only salute your brothers, what do you do more *than others do?* Do not even the publicans do this? Be therefore perfect, even as your Father who is in heaven is perfect.

20. Take heed that you do not give your alms before men, to be seen of them. Otherwise, you will have no reward from your Father who is in heaven. Therefore, when you give *your* alms, do not sound a trumpet before you, as the

hypocrites do in the synagogues and in the streets, that they may have glory from men. Verily, I say to you, they have their reward. However, when you give alms, do not let your left hand know what your right hand does so that your alms may be given in secret: and your Father who sees in your secret heart will reward you openly.

21. And when you pray, you do not be as the hypocrites *are* for they love to pray standing in the synagogues and on the corners of the streets, so that they may be seen by men. Verily, I say unto you, they have their reward. But you, when you pray, enter into your closet, and when you have shut your door, pray to your Father who is in your heart; and your Father who sees in secret will reward you openly. But when you pray, do not use vain repetitions, as the heathen *do:* for they think that they will be heard for their plentiful speaking. Therefore, do not be like them: for your Father knows what things you have need of, before you ask him. therefore you should pray in this manner;

22. <u>"Our Father who art in heaven, Hallowed be thy name, thy kingdom come. Thy will be done in earth, as *it is* in heaven. Give us this day our daily bread. And forgive us our debts, as we forgive our debtors. And lead us not into temptation, but deliver us from evil: For thine is the kingdom, and the power, and the glory, forever. Amen."</u>

23. "For, if you forgive men their trespasses, your heavenly Father will also forgive you: But if you do not forgive others their trespasses, neither will your Father forgive your trespasses.

24. Moreover, when you fast, do not be as the hypocrites with a sad countenance: for they disfigure their faces that they

may appear to men to fast. Verily, I say to you, they have their reward. But you, when you fast, anoint your head, and wash your face; so that you might not appear to men as fasting , but fast unto your Father who is in secret places of your heart: and your Father, who sees within the secrets of your heart, will reward you openly.

25. Do not lay up treasures for yourselves upon earth, where moth and rust will corrupt, and where thieves break through and steal. But lay up for treasures in the heaven of your heart, where neither moth nor rust doth corrupt, and where thieves do not break through nor steal: For where your treasure is, there will your heart be also.

26. The light of the body is the eye: Therefore, if your eye sees with a single purpose, your whole body will be full of light. But if your eye is full of evil, your whole body will be full of darkness. If the light that is in you is darkness, how great *will* that darkness be!

27. No man can serve two masters: for either he will hate the one, and love the other; or else he will hold to the one, and despise the other. You cannot serve God and mammon. Therefore, I say unto you, take no thought for your life, what you will eat, or what you will drink or the youth of your body or what you will put on. Is not life more than food and the body more than clothes? Behold the birds of the air: they do not sow, neither do they reap, nor do they gather into barns; yet your heavenly Father still feeds them. Are you not so much better than they?

28. Which of you by taking thought can add one cubit unto his stature? And why do you make thoughts about clothes? Consider the lilies of the field, how they grow. They do not

toil; neither do they spin. And yet I say to you, that even Solomon in all his glory was not arrayed like one of these. Wherefore, if God so clothes the grass of the field, which is here today, and gone tomorrow, *will he* not also *clothe* you even more?

29. O, you of little faith? Take no thought, saying, what will we eat or, what will we drink, or how will we be clothed? (For after all these things do the Gentiles seek) For your heavenly Father knows that you have need of all these things. But first, seek the kingdom of God, and his righteousness; and all these things will be added unto you. Therefore, take no thought for tomorrow: for tomorrow will take thought for itself. Each day has its own measure of evil without you worrying about it.

30. Judge not, so that you will not be judged. For with whatever judgment you judge, you will be judged. With whatever measure you deserve, it will be measured out to you. And why do you behold the speck that is in your brother's eye, but consider not the beam that is in your own eye? How can you say to your brother, Let me pull out the speck out of your eye; but there is a beam in your own eye? You hypocrite, first cast out the beam in your own eye; and then will you see clearly to cast out the speck in your brother's eye.

31. Give not that which is holy unto the dogs, or cast your pearls before swine, lest they trample them under their feet, and turn and attack you.

32. Ask, and it will be given to you; seek, search and you will find; knock, and it will be opened unto you: For everyone who asks will receive; and he that seeks shall finds; and to

him that knocks it will be opened. What man is there of you, who if his son ask for bread, will he give him a stone? Or if he asks for a fish, will give him a serpent? If you then, even being evil, know how to give good gifts to your children, how much more will your Father, who is in heaven and in your heart, give good things to them that ask him? Therefore, regarding all things, whatever you wish that men should do to you, do you even so to them: for this is the law of the prophets.

33. Enter in at the straight gate: for wide *is* the gate, and broad *is* the way, that leads to destruction, and there are many who go in there: Because straight *is* the gate, and narrow *is* the way, that leads to life, and there will few be that find it.

34. Beware of false prophets, who come to you in sheep's clothing, but inwardly they are ravening wolves. You will know them by their fruits. Do men gather grapes from thorns, or figs from thistles? Even so, every good tree brings forth good fruit; but a corrupt tree brings forth evil fruit. A good tree cannot bring forth evil fruit; neither *can* a corrupt tree bring forth good fruit. Every tree that does not bring forth good fruit will be cut down, and cast into the fire. Likewise, it is by their fruit that men will be known.

35. Not everyone that says to me, 'Lord, Lord, I want to enter into the kingdom of heaven.' will enter except that he does the will of my Father who is in heaven. Many will say to me in that day, Lord, Lord, have we not prophesied in your name, and in your name have cast out devils, and in your name done many wonderful works? And then will I

profess to them, I never knew you: depart from me, you who work iniquity.

36. Therefore, whoever hears these sayings of mine, and does them, I liken him to a wise man, who built his house upon a rock: And the rain descended, and the floods came, and the winds blew, and beat upon that house; and it did not fall: for it was founded upon a rock. And everyone that hears these sayings of mine, and does not follow them, will be likened to a foolish man, who built his house upon the sand: And the rain descended, and the floods came, and the winds blew, and beat upon that house; and it fell: and great was the fall of it."

37. And it came to pass, when Jesus had ended these sayings, that the people were astonished at his doctrine: For he taught them as *one* having authority, and not as the scribes.

38. When he came down from the mountain, great multitudes followed him. There came a leper who worshipped him, saying, Lord, if you will, you can make me clean. And Jesus put forth his hand, and touched him, saying, "**I will it so; be clean!**" And immediately his leprosy was cleansed. Jesus said to him, "**See that you tell no man; but go your way, show yourself to the priest, and offer the gift that Moses commanded, for a testimony unto them**".

39. When Jesus entered into Capernaum, a Roman Centurion came to him beseeching him, Saying, 'Lord, my servant lies at home sick of the palsy, grievously tormented'. Jesus replied, "**I will come with you and heal him**". The centurion answered and said, 'Lord, I am not concerned that you should come under my roof: Just say the word, and my servant will be healed. For I am a man under authority,

having soldiers under me: and I say to this *man,* Go, and he goes; and to another, Come, and he comes; and to my servant, Do this, and he does it'.

40. When Jesus heard *it,* he marveled, and said to those who followed, **"Verily I say to you, I have not found so great faith, no, not in all of Israel. And I say to you, that many will come from the east and west, and will sit down with Abraham, and Isaac, and Jacob, in the kingdom of heaven. But the children of the kingdom will be cast out into outer darkness: there will be weeping and gnashing of teeth."** Jesus said to the centurion, **"Go your way, and as you have believed, so will be it done unto you"**. And his servant was healed in the same hour."

41. When Jesus came to Peter's house, he saw his wife's mother laid out, and sick of a fever. And he touched her hand, and the fever left her: and she arose, and ministered unto them.

42. When the evening came, they brought him many who were possessed with devils: and he cast out the spirits with *his* word, and healed all that were sick: So that what was spoken by Esaias, the prophet, should be fulfilled, which was, "He took our infirmities, and healed *our* sicknesses".

43. Now when Jesus saw great multitudes about him, he decided to depart to the other side of the sea of Galilee, and a certain scribe came, and said to him, Master, 'I will follow you wherever you go.' And Jesus said to him, **"The foxes have holes, and the birds of the air *have* nests; but the Son of man has not a place to lay *his* head"**. And another of his would be disciples said unto him, Lord, allow

me to first go and bury my father. But Jesus said to him, **"Follow me; and let the dead bury their dead"**.

44. When he boarded a ship, his disciples followed him. And, behold, there arose a great tempest in the sea, so much so that the ship was covered with the waves: but he was asleep. And his disciples came to *him,* and awoke him, saying, Lord, save us: we will perish. And he said to them, **"Why are you fearful, O you of little faith?"** Then he arose, and rebuked the winds and the sea; and there was a great calm, and the men marveled, saying, 'What manner of man is this, that even the winds and the sea obey him!'

45. When he arrived on other side into the country of the Gergesenes, he met two men possessed with devils, who came out of the tombs, in an exceedingly fierce manner, so that no man might pass by that way. Then they cried out, 'What have we to do with you, Jesus, you Son of God? Have you come here to torment us before the time? A good way off from them there was a herd of many swine feeding. Therefore, the devils pleaded him, saying, if you cast us out; allow us to go away into the herd of swine. And he said unto them, **"Go!"**

46. When the devils came out and went into the herd of swine: The whole herd of swine ran violently down a steep place into the sea, and perished in the waters and the herdsmen who kept them fled, and went their ways into the city, and told everything of what befell to those who were possessed of the devils. Then the whole city came out to see Jesus: and when they saw him, they pleaded with *him* to depart from their coasts.

47. He then entered into a ship, and passed over the waters and came into his own city. They then brought to him a man sick of the palsy, lying on a bed. Jesus seeing their faith said to the sick man with palsy; "**Son, be of good cheer; your sins are forgiven you**". Then certain of the scribes said within themselves, this *man* blasphemes. Jesus, knowing their thoughts said, "**Why do you think evil in your heart? For whether it is easier, to say,** *your* **sins be forgiven, or to say, Arise, and walk!**"
48. "**So that you may know that the Son of man has power on earth to forgive sins,**" (then said he to the man sick with the palsy,) "**Arise, take up your bed, and go home.**" And the man arose, and departed to his house. But when the multitudes saw *it,* they marveled, and glorified God, who had given such power to men.
49. When Jesus passed forth from there, he saw a man, named Matthew, sitting at the receipt of custom taxes: and he said unto him, "**Follow me!**" And Matthew arose, and followed him.
50. And it came to pass, as Jesus sat at meat in a certain house, many publicans and sinners came and sat down with him and his disciples. When the Pharisees saw *it,* they said to his disciples, 'Why does your Master eat with publicans and sinners?' However, when Jesus heard *that,* he said to them, "**Those who are whole do not need a physician, but they who are sick do. Go and learn what** *that* **means. I will have mercy, and not sacrifice: for I am not come to call the righteous, but sinners to repentance.**"
51. Then disciples of John the Baptist came to him, saying, 'Why do we and the Pharisees fast often, but your disciples do

not? And Jesus replied to them, **"Can the children of the bride chamber mourn, as long as the bridegroom is with them? But the day will come, when the bridegroom will be taken from them, and then they will fast. No man puts a piece of new cloth unto an old garment, for that which is put in to fill it up takes from the garment, and the tear is made worse. Neither do men put new wine into old bottles: else the bottles break, and the wine runs out, and the bottles perish: but they put new wine into new bottles, and both are preserved."**

52. While he spoke these things to them, there came a certain ruler, and worshipped him, saying, my daughter is even now dead, but come and lay your hand upon her, and she will live. Jesus arose, and followed him, and *so did* his disciples.

53. On the way, a woman, who was diseased with an issue of blood twelve years, came behind *him,* and touched the hem of his garment: For she said within herself, if I may but touch his garment, I will be whole. But Jesus turned him about, and when he saw her, he said, **"Daughter, be of good comfort; your faith has made you whole"**. And the woman was made whole from that hour. When Jesus came into the ruler's house, and saw the minstrels and the people making a noise, He said unto them, **"Give us space, the girl is not dead, she is sleeping"**. And they laughed and scorned him. But when the people were put out, he went in, and took her by the hand, and the girl arose, and the fame of that went abroad into all corners of that land.

54. And when Jesus departed from there, two blind men followed him, crying, and saying, '*You* Son of David, have mercy on us', and when he came into a house, the blind

men came to him: and Jesus said unto them, "**Do you believe that I am able to do this?**" They told him, Yes, Lord. Then he touched their eyes, saying, "**According to your faith be it unto you**". And their eyes were opened; and Jesus straightly charged them, saying, "**See *that* no man knows *of this*"** But they, when they were departed, spread his fame all through country.

55. As they left a man was brought before who was dumb and possessed with a devil. When the devil was cast out, the dumb man spoke: and the multitudes marveled, saying, There had never been such a thing seen in Israel. But the Pharisees said, 'He casts out devils through the prince of the devils.' But Jesus went about all the cities and villages, teaching in their synagogues, and preaching the gospel of the kingdom, and healing every sickness and every disease among the people.

56. But when he saw the multitudes that followed him, he was moved with compassion for them, because they fainted, and were scattered abroad, as sheep having no shepherd. Then he said to his disciples, "**The harvest truly *is* plenteous, but the laborers *are* few; therefore, pray to the Lord of the harvest, that he will send forth laborers into his harvest**".

57. He then called to *him* his twelve disciples, and gave them power, *against* unclean spirits, to cast them out, and to heal all manner of sickness and all manner of disease. The names of the twelve apostles are these; The first, Simon, who is called Peter, and Andrew his brother; James *the son* of Zebedee, and John his brother; Philip, and Bartholomew; Thomas, and Matthew the tax collector; James *the son* of

Alphaeus, and Lebbaeus, whose surname was Thaddaeus; Simon the Canaanite, and Judas Iscariot, who betrayed him.

58. Jesus sent forth these twelve, and commanded them, saying, "**Do not go into the way of the Gentiles, and not into *any* city of the Samaritans: But go rather to the lost sheep of the house of Israel. As you go, preach, saying, 'The kingdom of heaven is at hand.' Heal the sick, cleanse the lepers, and raise the dead, cast out devils: Freely you have received, freely give. Provide neither gold, nor silver, nor brass in your purses, or script for *your* journey. Take neither two coats, or shoes, or stout staves: for the workman is worthy of his meat.

59. And into whatever city or town you enter, enquire who in it is worthy; and reside there until you leave. And when you come into a house, salute it. And if the house is worthy, let your peace come upon it: but if it is not worthy, let your peace return to you. And whoever will not receive you, or hear your words, when you depart out of that house or city, shake off the dust of your feet. Verily, I say unto you, it will be more tolerable for the land of Sodom and Gomorra in the Day of Judgment, than for that city.

60. Behold, I send you forth as sheep in the midst of wolves: be you therefore wise as serpents, and harmless as doves. But beware of men: for they will deliver you up to the councils, and they will scourge you in their synagogues; and you will be brought before governors and kings for my sake, to testify for them and the Gentiles.

61. But when they deliver you up, take no thought how or what you will speak: for it will be given you in that same

hour what you will speak. For it is not you who speaks, but the Spirit of your Father who speaks in you. And the brother will deliver up the brother to death, and the father the child: and the children will rise up against *their* parents, and cause them to be put to death. And you will be hated of all *men* for my name's sake: but he that endures to the end will be saved. But when they persecute you in any city, flee you into another: for verily I say unto you, you will not have gone over the cities of Israel, before the Son of man comes.

62. The disciple is not above *his* master, nor the servant above his lord. It is enough for the disciple that he is as his master, and the servant as his lord. If they have called the master of the house Beelzebub, what more will they call them of his household? Therefore, fear them not: for there is nothing covered, that will not be revealed; or hid, that will not be known. What I tell you in darkness, speak that in light: and what you hear in the ear, preach that upon the housetops. And fear not those who kill the body, but are not able to kill the soul: but rather fear him who is able to destroy both soul and body in hell.

63. Are not two sparrows sold for a penny? And one of them will not fall on the ground without your Father knowing of it. The very hairs of your head are all numbered. Therefore, do not fear; you are of more value than any sparrow. Whoever will confess me before men, will I confess him also before my Father who is in heaven. But whoever will deny me before men, will I also deny him before my Father who is in heaven.

64. Do not think that I am come to bring peace on earth: I came not to send peace, but a sword. For I have come to set a man at variance against his father, and the daughter against her mother, and the daughter in law against her mother in law. And a man's foes *will be* his own household. He that loves their father or mother more than me is not worthy of me: and he that loves son or daughter more than me is not worthy of me. And he that does not take up his cross, and follow after me, is not worthy of me. He that finds his life will lose it: and he that loses his life for my sake will find it.

65. He that receives you receives me, and he that receives me receives him that sent me. He that receives a prophet in the name of a prophet will receive a prophet's reward; and he that receives a righteous man in the name of a righteous man will receive a righteous man's reward. And whoever will give to one of these little ones a cup of cold *water* to drink only in the name of a disciple, verily I say unto you, he will in no way lose his reward."

66. And so it happened, that when Jesus finished commanding his twelve disciples, he departed to teach and to preach in their cities. Now when John the Baptist had heard in the prison the works of Christ, he sent two of his disciples, and said unto him, Are you He that should come, or do we look for another? Jesus answered and said to them, "**Go and show John again those things which you hear and see:** The blind receive their sight, the lame walk, the lepers are cleansed, the deaf hear, the dead are raised, the poor have the gospel preached to them and blessed is *he* whoever will not be offended in me."

67. And as they departed, Jesus began to speak to the multitudes concerning John the Baptist, "**What did you go out into the wilderness to see? A reed shaken with the wind? What did you go out to see? A man clothed in soft raiment?** Behold, they that wear soft *clothing* are in kings' houses. But what did you go out to see? A prophet? Yes, I say to you, 'He was more than a prophet'. For this is *he,* of whom it is written, Behold, I send my messenger before your face, who will prepare your way before you.

68. Verily I say unto you, among them who are born of women there has not risen a greater than John the Baptist: notwithstanding that the least in the kingdom of heaven is greater than John. And from the days of John the Baptist until now, the kingdom of heaven suffers violence, and the violent take it by force. For all the prophets and the law prophesied until John. And if you will receive *it,* this is Elias, who was to come. He that has ears to hear, let him hear.

69. However, to what will I liken this generation? They are like children sitting in the markets, and calling to their fellows, and saying, we have piped to you, and you have not danced. We have mourned for you, and you have not lamented. For John came neither eating nor drinking, and they say, He has a devil. The Son of man came eating and drinking, and they say, Behold a gluttonous man, and a wine-swiller, a friend of publicans and sinners. But wisdom is justified of her children."

70. Then he began to upbraid the cities wherein most of his mighty works were done, because they did not repent. "**Woe unto you, Chorazin! Woe unto you, Bethsaida!** For if the mighty works, which were done in you, had been done in Tyre and Sidon they would have repented long ago in sackcloth and ashes. But I say to you, it will be more tolerable for Tyre and Sidon at the Day of Judgment, than for you. And you, Capernaum, which is exalted unto heaven, will be brought down to hell: for if the mighty works, which have been done in you, had been done in Sodom, it would have remained until this day. But I say to you, that it will be more tolerable for the land of Sodom in the Day of Judgment, than for you."

71. At that time, Jesus prayed and said, "I thank you, O Father, Lord of heaven and earth, because you have hid these things from the wise and prudent, and have revealed them unto babes. Even so, Father, for so it seemed good in your sight. All things are delivered to me from my Father: and no man knows the Son, but the Father; neither does any man know the Father, save the Son, and *he* to whomever the Son will reveal *him.*

72. Come to me, all *you* that labor and are heavy laden, and I will give you rest. Take my yoke upon you, and learn of me; for I am meek and lowly in heart: and you will find rest unto your souls. For my yoke *is* easy, and my burden is light."

73. At that time, Jesus went on the Sabbath day through the grain; and his disciples were hungry, and began to pluck the grain, and to eat. But when the Pharisees saw *it* they said to him, look; your disciples do that which is not lawful to do upon the Sabbath day. At which he said to them, "**Have you not read what David did, when he was hungry, and they that were with him; How he entered into the house of**

God, and ate the showbread, which was not lawful for him to eat, nor for them who were with him, but only for the priests? Or, have you not read in the law, how on the Sabbath days the priests in the temple profane the Sabbath, and are blameless?

74. But I say to you that in this place there is *one* greater than the temple. But if you had known what *this* meant, I would have received mercy, and not been sacrificed, and you would not have condemned the guiltless. For the Son of man is Lord even of the Sabbath day." And when he left there he went into their synagogue:

75. And, behold, there was a man who had *his* hand withered. The priests asked of Jesus, saying, 'Is it lawful to heal on the Sabbath days?' So that they might accuse him and he said to them, **"What man will there be among you, who has a sheep, and if it falls into a pit on the Sabbath day, will he not lay hold on it, and lift *it* out? How much then is a man better than a sheep? Therefore it is lawful to do good on the Sabbath days"**. Then he said to the man, **"Stretch forth your hand"**. And he stretched *it* forth; and it was restored whole, like the other.

76. Then the Pharisees left, and held a council against him, on how they might destroy him. But when Jesus knew *it,* he withdrew from there, and great multitudes followed him, and he healed them all. Then he told them, **"That they should not make him known, so that it might be fulfilled which was spoken by Esaias the prophet. Who said, 'Behold my servant, who I have chosen; my beloved, in whom my soul is well pleased: I will put my spirit upon him, and he will show judgment to the Gentiles. He will**

not strive, nor cry; neither will any man hear his voice in the streets. A bruised reed he will not break, and smoking flax he will not quench, until he sends forth judgment unto victory, and in his name will the Gentiles trust'."

77. Then there was brought to him one possessed with a devil, blind, and dumb: and he healed him, so much so that the blind and dumb man both spoke and saw, and all the people were amazed, and said, Is not this the son of David? But when the Pharisees heard *it,* they said, this *fellow* does not cast out devils, except by Beelzebub the prince of the devils.

78. However, Jesus knew their thoughts, and he said to them, **"Every kingdom divided against itself is brought to desolation; and every city or house divided against itself will not stand: And if Satan casts out Satan, he is divided against himself; how will then his kingdom stand? And if I by Beelzebub cast out devils, by whom do your children cast *them* out? Therefore, they will be your judges. But if I cast out devils by the Spirit of God, then the kingdom of God is come unto you. Likewise, how can one enter into a strong man's house, and spoil his goods, except he first binds the strong man? And then spoil his house."** Then Jesus said, **"He that is not with me is against me; and he that gathers not with me scatters abroad"**.

79. "Therefore, I say to you, all manner of sin and blasphemy will be forgiven when done to men: but the blasphemy *against* the *Holy* Ghost will not be forgiven. And who ever speaks a word against the Son of man, it will be forgiven him: but who ever speaks against the Holy Ghost, it will not be forgiven him, neither in this world, nor in the *world* to come.

80. Either call the tree good, and its fruit good; or else call the tree corrupt, and its fruit corrupt: for a tree is known by its fruit. O, generation of vipers, how can you, being evil, speak good things? For out of the abundance of the heart the mouth speaks. A good man out of the good treasure of the heart brings forth good things: and an evil man out of the evil treasure brings forth evil things. But I say unto you, that for every idle word that men will speak, they will have to give account of in the Day of Judgment. For by your words you will be justified, and by your words you will be condemned."

81. Then certain of the scribes and of the Pharisees answered, saying, 'Master, we would like to see a sign from you.' He answered them saying to them, "**An evil and adulterous generation seeks after a sign, and there will no sign be given to it, but the sign of the prophet Jonas. For as Jonas was three days and three nights in the whale's belly; so will the Son of man be three days and three nights in the heart of the earth.**

82. **The men of Nineveh will rise up in judgment of this generation, and will condemn it, because they have repented on hearing the preaching of Jonas. But behold a greater one than Jonas** *is* **here. The queen of Sheba will rise up in judgment of this generation, and will condemn it, for she came from the uttermost parts of the earth to hear the Wisdom of Solomon. But behold one greater than Solomon** *is* **here.**

83. **When the unclean spirit leaves a man, it walks through dry places, seeking rest, and finds none. When it says, I will return to the place from where I came. And when it comes home to the man, it finds** *it* **empty, swept, and garnished. When the evil spirit leaves it takes with it seven other spirits more wicked than itself, and they enter into another man and dwell there: and the state of this man is worse than the first. Even so will it be unto this wicked generation also."**

84. While he so talked to the people, behold, *his* mother and his brothers stood outside, desiring to speak with him. Then someone said unto him, Behold, your mother and your brothers stand outside, desiring to speak with you. But he answered and said to him that told him, **"Who is my mother? And who are my brothers?"** And he stretched forth his hand toward his disciples, and said, **"Behold my mother and my brothers! For whoever does the will of my Father who is in heaven, is the same as my brother, and sister, and mother."**

85. The same day went Jesus out of the house, and sat by the seaside, and great multitudes gathered together around him. So he went aboard a ship, and sat down, and the whole multitude stood on the shore. And he spoke many things unto them in parables, saying, **"Behold, a farmer went forth to sow; and when he sowed, some** *seeds* **fell by the way side, and the fowls came and devoured them. Some fell upon stony places, where there was not much earth: and forthwith they sprung up, because they had no deepness of earth, and when the sun came up, they were scorched because they had no root, and they withered**

away. Some seeds fell among thorns, and the thorns sprung up, and choked them: But other seeds fell onto good ground, and brought forth fruit, some a hundredfold, some sixtyfold, some thirtyfold". Then he said, "He who has ears to hear, let him hear this"

86. His disciples came, and said to him, 'Why do you speak to them in parables?' He answered and said to them, "**Because it is given unto you to know the mysteries of the kingdom of heaven, but to them it is not given. For whoever has, to him it will be given, and he will have more in abundance: but whoever has not, from him will be taken away even that which he has.**

87. Therefore, I speak to them in parables because although they look, they do not see, and though they listen, they do not hear, neither do they understand, and in them is fulfilled the prophecy of Esaias which says, 'By hearing you will hear, but will not understand; and seeing you will see, but will not perceive.' Because of this people's hearts grow heavy, and *their* ears are dull of hearing, and their eyes have closed, unless at any time they should see with *their* eyes, and hear with *their* ears, and should understand with *their* heart, and should be converted, and I should heal them.

88. But blessed *are* the eyes of my disciples, for they see, and your ears, for they hear. For verily I say unto you, That many prophets and righteous *men* have desired to see *those things* which you see, and have not seen *them;* and to hear *those things* which you hear, and have not heard *them.*

89. Therefore, listen to the parable of the sower. When any one hears the word of the kingdom, and does not understand *it*, then the wicked *one* comes, and catches away that which was sown in his heart. This is he who received seed by the way side.
90. But he that received the seed into stony places is the same as the one that hears the word, and now with joy receives it. But just as has he no root in himself, but endures for only a while, because when tribulation or persecution arises because of the Word, by and by he loses track of the word.
91. He that received seed among the thorns is he that hears the word, but because of the cares of this world, and the deceitfulness of riches that choke the word, he becomes unfruitful.
92. But he that received seed into the good ground is the one that hears the word, and understands *it*. It is he who bears fruit, and brings forth, sometimes a hundredfold, sometimes sixty, sometimes thirty."
93. He put forth another parable to them, saying, "**The kingdom of heaven is likened unto a man who sowed good seed in his field:** But while the man slept, his enemy came and sowed weeds among the wheat, and went his way. But when the wheat sprung up, and brought forth fruit, then the weeds appeared also. So the servants of the householder came and said to him, Sir, you must have not sown good seed in your field? Where did the weeds come from? He said unto them, an enemy has done this to me.
94. The servants then said to him, 'Do you want us to go and gather them up'? But he said, No, because while you

gather up the weeds, you might root up the wheat with them too. Let them both grow together until the harvest: and in the time of harvest I will say to the reapers, first gather together the weeds, and bind them in bundles and burn them: then gather the wheat into the barn."

95. Another parable he put forth to them, saying, "**The kingdom of heaven is like a mustard seed, which a man took and sowed in his field. Which indeed is the least of all seeds: but when it is grown, it is the greatest among herbs, and becomes a tree, so that the birds of the air come and lodge in its branches.**"

96. He told them another parable; "**The kingdom of heaven is like yeast, which a woman took, and kneaded into three measures of meal, till the whole was leavened.**"

97. Jesus spoke to the multitude in parables about all these things; Everything he said to them was in parables; so that it might fulfill that which was spoken of by the prophet, saying, "**I will open my mouth in parables; I will utter things which have been kept secret from the foundation of the world.**" Then Jesus sent the multitude away, and went into the house, and his disciples came to him, saying, Explain to us the parable of the weeds of the field.

98. He answered and said to them, "**He that sows the good seed is the Son of man. The field is the world. The good seed are the children of the kingdom; but the weeds are the children of the wicked** *one;* **the enemy that sowed them is the devil; the harvest is the end of the world; and the reapers are the angels.**

99. Therefore as the weeds are gathered and burned in the fire; so will it be in the end of this world. The Son of man

will send forth his angels, and they will gather out of his kingdom all those who offend, and they who do evil; And will cast them into a furnace of fire: there will be wailing and gnashing of teeth. Then the righteous will shine forth as the sun in the kingdom of their Father. He who has ears to hear, let him hear!

100. Again, the kingdom of heaven is like a treasure hid in a field; which, when a man has found it, he hides, and out of joy, he goes and sells all that he has, and buys that field.

101. Again, the kingdom of heaven is like a merchant, seeking goodly pearls: Who, when he had found one pearl of great price, went and sold all that he had, and bought it.

102. Again, the kingdom of heaven is like a net, that was cast into the sea, and gathered of every kind, which, when it was full, they drew to shore, and sat down, and gathered the good into vessels, and cast the bad away. So will it be at the end of the world: the angels will come forth, and sever the wicked from among the just, and will cast them into the furnace of fire: there will be wailing and gnashing of teeth." Then Jesus said to them, "**Have you understood all these things?**" They said in reply, 'Yes, Lord.' Then he said to them, "**Therefore, every wise man *who is* inducted into the kingdom of heaven is like a man *that is* a householder, who brings forth out of his treasure *things* both new and old.**"

103. And it came to pass, *that* when Jesus had finished these parables, he departed and when he returned to his own country, he taught in the synagogue, so much so that they were astonished, and said, 'Where has this *man* acquired this wisdom, and *these* mighty works? Is not this the

carpenter's son, is not his mother called Mary, and his brothers, James, and Joses, and Simon, and Judas and his sisters, are they not all with us? Where then has this *man* learned of all these things?' They were offended by him, but Jesus responded to them saying, "**A prophet is honored everywhere, except in his own country, and in his own house.**" And he did not do many mighty works there because of their unbelief.

104. At that time Herod the tetrarch heard of the fame of Jesus, and said to his servants, 'This is John the Baptist; he is risen from the dead, therefore mighty works show forth in him.'

105. For Herod had arrested John, and bound him, and put *him* in prison to please Herodias', his brother Philip's wife, because John had told him that It was not lawful for him to marry his brother's wife. When Herod wanted to have put him to death, he did not, because he feared the multitude, because they counted John as a prophet.

106. But when Herod's birthday came, the daughter of Herodias, danced before them, and pleased Herod. Whereupon he promised with an oath to give her, whatever she would ask. Then she, being instructed before, by her mother, said, 'Give me John the Baptist's head on a plate.' Herod was sorry: nevertheless, because of the oath, and the regard them who dined with, he commanded that her wish be granted. He sent his men to beheaded John in prison and bring his head in on a plate, which was then given to the young woman, and she brought *it* to her mother. Afterward, John's disciples came, and took up the body, and buried it, and went and told Jesus.

107. When Jesus heard *about it,* he left by ship to a desert place apart: and when the people heard *about it,* they followed him on foot out of the cities. And Jesus went forth, and saw a great multitude, and was moved with compassion toward them, and he healed their sick.

108. When dusk arrived, his disciples came to him, saying, 'This is a desert place, and the time is now late, send the multitude away, so that they may go into the villages, and buy food.' But Jesus said to them, **"They need not depart; give them something to eat."** And they said to him, 'We only have five loaves, and two fish.' He replied, **"Bring them here to me"**.

109. He commanded the multitude to sit down on the grass, and took the five loaves, and the two fish, and looking up to heaven, he blessed, and broke them. Then he gave the loaves to *his* disciples, and the disciples gave them to the multitude, and they all ate, and were filled. They took up of the fragments that remained which were twelve baskets full. They that had eaten were about five thousand men, including women and children.

110. Straightway Jesus ordered his disciples to get into a ship, and to go before him to the other side, while he sent the multitudes away. When he had sent the multitudes away, he went up into a mountain apart, to pray, and when the evening came, he was there alone. But the ship was now in the midst of the sea, tossed with waves: for the wind was contrary, and in the fourth watch of the night, Jesus went to them, walking on the sea. When the disciples saw him walking on the sea, they were troubled, saying, 'It is a

spirit! And they cried out in fear. But right way Jesus spoke unto them, saying, "**Be of good cheer; it is I; be not afraid**".

111. Peter answered him and said, 'Lord, if it is really you; let me come to you on the water.' Jesus said, "**Come**", and when Peter came down out of the ship, he walked on the water, to go to Jesus, but when he felt the boisterous wind, he was afraid. Beginning to sink, he cried out, saying, 'Lord, save me!' Immediately Jesus stretched forth his hand, and caught him, and said to him, "**O you of little faith, why did you doubt?**" When they returned to the ship, the wind ceased, and the others who were in the ship came and worshipped him, saying, truly, you are the Son of God.

112. When they had passed over the waters, they came to the land of Gennesaret, and when the men of that place knew of his presence, they sent word out into all that country round about, and brought to him all that were diseased. They only asked that they might touch the hem of his garment, and all who touched it were made perfect and whole.

113. Then scribes and Pharisees, from Jerusalem arrived, saying, 'Why do your disciples transgress the tradition of the elders?' They do not wash their hands when they eat bread. He replied and said unto them, "**Why do you also transgress the commandment of God by your tradition? For God commanded, saying, Honor your father and mother: and, He that curses father or mother, let him die the death. But you say, 'whoever will say to his father or his mother, 'It is a gift of God, whatever you might profit from me', does not have to honor his mother and father at**

all if the gift is to the synagogue', Thus have you made the commandment of God of no effect by your tradition.

114. *You* hypocrites, well did Esaias prophesy of you, saying, 'These people draws near to me with their mouths, and honor me with *their* lips; but their hearts are far from me.' But in vain do they worship me, teaching *as* if they were Laws of God, the commandments of men."

115. And he called the multitude, and said to them, **"Hear, and understand: That which goes into the mouth does not defile a man; but that which comes out of the mouth, this defiles a man."** Then his disciples came, and they said to him, you do know that the Pharisees were offended after they heard this saying? He answered them and said, **"Every plant, which my heavenly Father has not planted, will be rooted up."** Let them alone: they are blind men who lead the blind. And if the blind lead the blind, both will fall into the ditch."

116. Then Peter replied and said to him, 'Explain this parable to us.' Jesus said, **"Are you also without understanding? Do you not understand that whatever enters in at the mouth goes into the belly, and is cast out into the sewer? But those things that proceed out of the mouth come forth from the heart; and this is what defiles a man. Because, it is from the heart that evil thoughts, murders, adulteries, fornications, thefts, false witness, and blasphemies proceed: These are *the things* that defile a man: eating with unwashed hands does not defile a man."**

117. Then Jesus left for the coasts of Tire and Sidon. And, behold, a woman of Canaan came out of the same coasts, and cried out to him, saying, 'Have mercy on me, O Lord,

you Son of David; my daughter is grievously vexed with a devil.' But he answered her not a word. And his disciples came and pleaded with him, saying; 'Send her away; for she cries after us.' But he answered and said, "**I am not sent, except to the lost sheep of the house of Israel.**" Then she came forward and worshipped him, saying, 'Lord, help me'. Jesus challenged her and said, "**It is not right to take the children's bread, and to cast *it* to dogs**." She responded, 'Truly so, Lord! Yet the dogs eat of the crumbs that fall from their masters' table'. Jesus looked at her and said, "**O woman, great *is* your faith: be it unto you even as you wish. And her daughter was made whole from that very hour.**"

118. Jesus departed from that place, and came to the Sea of Galilee, and went up onto a mountain, and sat down there. And great multitudes came to him, bringing with them *those who were* lame, blind, dumb, maimed, and many others, and sat them down at Jesus' feet. And he healed them: so much that the multitude was amazed when they saw the dumb to speak, the maimed made whole, the lame to walk, and the blind to see, that they glorified the God of Israel.

119. Then Jesus called his disciples *to him,* and said, "**I have compassion on the multitude, because they continue with me now three days, and have had nothing to eat: and I will not send them away fasting, because they might faint on the way.**" His disciples said to him, 'Where should we get so much bread in the wilderness to feed so great a multitude?' And Jesus said to them, "**How many loaves do you have? And they said, seven, and a few little fish.**"

120. And he commanded the multitude to sit down on the ground. And he took the seven loaves and the fish, and gave thanks, and broke *them,* and gave them to his disciples, and the disciples to the multitude. And they all ate, and were filled: and they took up seven baskets full of the broken *meat* that was left. And there were four thousand men, beside women and children who were fed. Then he sent the multitude away, and boarded a ship, and set sail for the coast of Magdala.

121. The Pharisees and the Sadducees came, and tempted him, asking him to show them a sign from heaven. He answered and said to them, "**When it is evening, you say,** *it will be* **fair weather: for the sky is red. And in the morning,** *it will be* **foul weather today: for the sky is red and lowering. O,** *you* **hypocrites, you can discern the face of the sky, but can you not** *discern* **the signs of the times? A wicked and adulterous generation seeks after a sign, but there will no sign be given unto it, but the sign of the prophet Jonas."** And he left them, and departed. And when his disciples came from the other side of the sea, they had forgotten to bring bread.

122. Jesus then said to them, "**Take heed and beware of the leaven of the Pharisees and of the Sadducees**". The disciples reasoned among themselves, saying, *Is it* because we have brought no bread? *When* Jesus perceived what they were thinking, he said to them, "**Oh, you of little faith, why reason among yourselves, because you have brought no bread? Do you not understand, or even remember, the five loaves of the five thousand, or how many baskets you took up? Or either the seven loaves of the four thousand,**

or how many baskets you took up? How is it that you do not understand that I did not speak to you concerning bread, but that you should become aware of the leaven of the Pharisees and of the Sadducees?"** Then they understood that what he told *them* was not about bread, but of the doctrines of the Pharisees and of the Sadducees.

123. When Jesus came to the coasts of Caesarea Philippi, he asked his disciples, saying, **"Who do men say that I, the Son, of Man am?"** And they said, some *say that you are* John the Baptist: some say Elias; and others, Jeremias, or one of the prophets. He questioned them further, **"But who do you say that I am?"** And Simon Peter answered and said, 'You are the Christ, the Son of the living God.' And Jesus answered and said to him, **"Blessed are you, Simon Barjona: for flesh and blood has not revealed** *it* **unto you, but my Father which is in heaven. And I say to you, that you, who are called Peter, will be the rock upon which I will build my church; and the gates of hell will not prevail against it. And I will give unto you the keys of the kingdom of heaven: and whatever you will bind on earth will be bound in heaven: and whatever you will loose on earth will be loosed in heaven."** Then he charged his disciples that they should tell no man that he is Jesus the Christ.

124. From that time forth Jesus began to describe to his disciples, how he must go into Jerusalem, and suffer many things of the elders and chief priests and scribes, and be killed, and be raised again the third day. Then Peter took him, and began to rebuke him, saying, 'be it far from you, Lord: this will not be done to you'. But Jesus turned, and said to Peter, **"Get behind me, Satan: you are an offence**

unto me: for you do not savor the things that be of God, but those things that be of men."

125. Then Jesus said to his disciples, "**If any *man* will come after me, let him deny himself, and take up his cross, and follow me. For whoever will save his life will lose it: and who ever will lose his life for my sake will find it. For what does a man profit, if he will gain the whole world, and then lose his own soul? Or what will a man give in exchange for his soul? For the Son of man will come in the glory of his Father with his angels; and then he will reward every man according to his works. Verily, I say unto you, there are some standing here, who will not taste of death, till they see the Son of man coming in his kingdom."**

126. And after six days Jesus, along with Peter, James, and John his brother, climbed up onto a high mountain and was transfigured before them: and his face shone as the sun, and his were as white as light. And, behold, there appeared unto them Moses and Elias talking with him.

127. Then Peter said to Jesus, 'Lord, it is good for us to be here: if you will, let us make here three tabernacles, one for you, and one for Moses, and one for Elias'. While he thus spoke, behold, a bright cloud overshadowed them: and behold a voice came out of the cloud, and said, 'This is my beloved Son, in whom I am well pleased; listen to him.' When the disciples heard *it,* they fell on their face, and were very afraid.

128. And Jesus came and touched them, and said, "**Arise, friends, and be not afraid."** And when they lifted up their eyes, they saw no one, except Jesus. And as they came down from the mountain, Jesus charged them, saying, "**Tell**

this vision to no man, until the Son of man be risen again from the dead".

129. His disciples then asked him, 'Why do the scribes say that Elias must first come?' **But I tell you, that Elias has come already, but they did not recognize him, and did to him whatever they wanted. Likewise, will the Son of man experience the same from them."** Then the disciples understood that he was speaking to them about John the Baptist.

130. When they came before the multitude, a *certain* man came to him, kneeling down to him, and saying, 'Lord, have mercy on my son, he is lunatic, and very troubled: for often he falls into the fire, and often into the water. I brought him to your disciples, but they could not cure him'. Jesus answered, **"O faithless and perverse generation, how long will I be with you? How long will I suffer with you? Bring him here to me."** And Jesus rebuked the devil; and he departed out of him: and the child was cured from that very hour.

131. When Jesus and the disciples were alone, they asked him, 'Why could we not cast him out?' Jesus said to them, **"Because of your unbelief: for verily, I say unto you, if you have faith as a grain of mustard seed, and you say to this mountain, Move to yonder place; it will move. Nothing will be impossible for you. Although, this kind of affliction only goes away with much prayer and fasting."**

132. And while they stayed in Galilee, Jesus said to them, **"The Son of man will be betrayed into the hands of men: And they will kill him, and on the third day he will be raised again."** And they were exceedingly sorry.

133. And when they came to Capernaum, the tax collectors came to Peter, and said, 'Does your master pay tribute?' Peter said, 'Yes', and when he came into the house, Jesus stopped him, saying, **"What do you think, Simon? From whom do the kings of the earth take custom or tribute? From their own children or from strangers?"** Jesus said to him, **"Therefore, the children are free of tribute. But, unless we should offend them, go to the sea, and cast in a hook, and take up the first fish that comes up; and when you have opened his mouth, you will find a piece of money: take that and give it to them for me and you."**

134. At the same time the disciples came to Jesus, saying, who is the greatest in the kingdom of heaven? And Jesus called a little child to him, and set him in the midst of them, And said, **"Verily, I say unto you, Except that you are converted, and become as little children, you will not enter into the kingdom of heaven. Therefore, whoever will humble himself as this little child, the same is greatest in the kingdom of heaven. And whoever will receive one such little child in my name receives me. But whoever will offend one of these little ones who believe in me, it were better for him that a millstone were hanged about his neck, and *that* he were drowned in the depth of the sea.**

135. **Woe unto the world because of such offences! For it must be that such offences come, but woe to that man from whom the offence comes! Wherefore if your hand or your foot offends you, cut them off, and cast *them* from you: it is better for you to enter into life halt or maimed, rather than having two hands or two feet and be cast into everlasting fire. And if your eye offend you, pluck it out,**

and cast *it* from you: it is better for you to enter into life with one eye, rather than having two eyes and be cast into hell fire.

136. Take heed that you despise not one of these little ones, for I say unto you, that in heaven their angels do always behold the face of my Father who is in heaven. For the Son of man has come to save that which was lost. What do you think? If a man has a hundred sheep, and one of them goes astray, does he not leave the ninety-nine, and go into the mountains and seeks that which is gone astray? And if it happens that he finds it, verily I say to you, he rejoices more for that one *sheep,* than for the ninety and nine that did not go astray. Even so, it is not the will of your Father, who is in heaven, that one of these little ones should perish.

137. Moreover, if your brother trespasses against you, go and tell him his fault between you and him alone: if he will hear you, you have gained your brother. But if he will not hear *you, then* take with you one or two more people, so that in the mouth of two or three witnesses every word may be established.

138. And if he neglects to hear them, tell *it* in the church: but if he neglects to hear the church, let him be to you as a heathen man and a publican. Verily, I say unto you, whatever you will bind on earth will be bound in heaven: and whatever you will loose on earth will be loosed in heaven. Again, I say unto you, that if two of you will agree on earth as to anything that they will ask, it will be done for them of my Father who is in heaven. For where two or

three are gathered together in my name, there am I in the midst of them."

139. Then came Peter to him, and said, 'Lord, how often must my brother sin against me, and I forgive him? Till seven times?' Jesus said to him, "**I say to you, not seven times: but, until seventy times seven.**"

140. "Therefore is the kingdom of heaven likened unto a certain king, who would take account of his servants. And when he had begun to reckon, one was brought to him, who owed him ten talents. But because he had nothing to pay, his lord commanded him to be sold, and his wife, and children, and all that he had, and payment to be made. The servant therefore fell down, and worshipped him, saying, Lord, have patience with me, and I will pay you all. Then the lord of that servant was moved with compassion and excused him, and forgave him the debt.

141. But the same servant went out, and found one of his fellow servants, who owed him an hundred pence: and he laid hands on him, and took *him* by the throat, saying, Pay me what you owe me! And his fellow servant fell down at his feet, and pleaded with him, saying, have patience with me, and I will pay everything. But he would not forgive the debt: and went and cast the fellow servant into prison, until he could pay the debt.

142. So when his fellow servants saw what was done, they were very sorry, and came and told their lord all that had happened. Then his lord, after he had called him, said to him, O, you wicked servant, I forgave you all that debt, because you begged me: Should you not also have had compassion on your fellow servant, even as I had pity on

you? But his lord was wrathful, and delivered him to the bill collectors, until he could pay all that was due unto him. So likewise will my heavenly Father do also to you, if you, from your heart, cannot forgive everyone their trespasses."

143. And it came to pass, *that* when Jesus had finished these sayings, he departed from Galilee, and came into the coasts of Judaea beyond Jordan; and great multitudes followed him; and he healed them there.

144. The Pharisees also came to him, tempting him, and saying to him, 'Is it lawful for a man to put away his wife for any cause'? And he answered and said unto them, "**Have you not read, that he who made** *them* **at the beginning made them male and female, And said, For this cause will a man leave father and mother, and will cleave to his wife: and the two will become one flesh? Where they are no more two, but one flesh. What God has joined together, let not man put asunder.**"

145. They said to him, 'Then why did Moses command the writing of writs of divorcement, that allows a wife to be put away'? He said to them, "**Moses, because of the hardness of your heart, allowed you to put away your wives: but from the beginning, it was not so. And I say to you, whoever puts away his wife, except for adultery, and marries again commits adultery: and whoever marries her who is divorced also commits adultery.**"

146. His disciples said to him, 'If that is the case regarding a man with *a* wife, then it is not good to marry'. But he explained to them, "**All** *men* **cannot receive this saying, except** *those* **to whom it is given. For there are some**

eunuchs, who were so born from *their* mother's womb: and there are some eunuchs, who were made eunuchs by men: and there are eunuchs, who have made themselves celibate for the kingdom of heaven's sake. He that is able to receive *it,* let him receive *it.*"

147. Then little children were there brought to him so that he could put *his* hands on them, and pray, and the disciples rebuked the ones who brought the children to be blessed. But Jesus said, "**Suffer the little children, and do not forbid them to come to me: for of such is the kingdom of heaven.**" And he laid *his* hands on them, and then departed.

148. Then a young man came and said to him, Good Master, what good thing will I do, that I may have eternal life? Jesus said to him, "**Why do you call me good?** *There is* **none good but one,** *that is,* **God: but if you will enter into life, keep the commandments.**" The man asked him, 'Which commandments?' Jesus said, "**You shall not murder. You shall not commit adultery. You shall not steal. You shall not bear false witness. You shall honor your father and** *your* **mother: and you must love your neighbor as yourself.**"

149. The young man said to him, 'all these things have I kept from my youth up: What else do I need to do?' Jesus said unto him, "**If you wish be perfect, go** *and* **sell that you have, and give to the poor, and you will have treasure in heaven, and come** *and* **follow me**". But when the young man heard that saying, he went away sorrowful: for he had great possessions.

150. Then said Jesus to his disciples, **Verily, I say unto you, it will be difficult for a rich man to enter into the kingdom of heaven. And again I say to you, it would be easier for a camel to go through the eye of a needle, than for a rich man to enter into the kingdom of God."** When his disciples heard *it,* they were exceedingly amazed, saying, 'Who then can be saved?' But Jesus beheld *them,* and said to them, **"With men this is impossible; but with God all things are possible".**

151. Then answered Peter and said unto him, Behold, we have forsaken all, and followed you; what will we have therefore? And Jesus said to them, **"Verily, I say to you, that you who have followed me, in the regeneration when the Son of man will sit in the throne of his glory, you also will sit upon twelve thrones, judging the twelve tribes of Israel. And everyone that has forsaken houses, or brothers, or sisters, or father, or mother, or wife, or children, or lands, for my name's sake, will receive a hundredfold, and will inherit everlasting life. But many** *that are* **first will be last; and the last** *will be* **first."**

152. **"For the kingdom of heaven can be likened unto a man** *that is* **a householder, who went out early in the morning to hire laborers in his vineyard. When he had agreed with the laborers for a penny a day, he sent them into his vineyard. When he went out about the third hour, and saw others standing idle in the marketplace, and said to them; Go into the vineyard also, and whatever is right I will give you. And they went their way. Again, he went out about the sixth and ninth hour, and did likewise. About the last minute, he went out and found others standing idle, and**

said to them, why stand here all the day idle? They said to him, because no man has hired us. He told them, Go also into the vineyard; and whatever is right, you will receive. So when evening came, the lord of the vineyard said to his steward, Call the laborers, and give them *their* wages, beginning from the last unto the first. And when those were *were hired* in the eleventh hour came forth they each received a penny. But when the first hired came, they supposed that they should receive more; but they likewise also received a penny. When they received it, they murmured against the good man of the house, Saying, These last hired have worked *but* one hour, and you have made them equal to us who have borne the burden and heat of the day. But he answered one of them, and said, Friend, I did you no wrong: did not you agree with me for a penny? Take *that* which is yours, and go your way: I will give to these last, even as to you. Is it not lawful for me to do what I want with my own money? Is your eye evil, because I am good?" Jesus concluded by saying, "The last will be first and the first the last: for many are called, but few are chosen."

153. And Jesus, on the way to Jerusalem, took the twelve disciples apart and said to them, "**Behold, we go up to Jerusalem. The Son of man will be betrayed by the chief priests and the scribes, and they will condemn him to death, and they will deliver him to the Gentiles to mock, and to scourge, and to crucify** *him:* **and on the third day he will rise again."**

154. Then the mother of Zebedee's children came to him with her sons, worshipping *him,* and desiring a certain thing

of him. He asked her, **"What do you wish?"** She said to him, 'Grant that these, my two sons, may sit, the one on your right hand, and the other on the left, in your kingdom'. But Jesus smiled and said, **"You do not know what you are asking. Are you able to drink of the cup that I will drink of, and to be baptized with the baptism that I am baptized with?"** Her sons said to him, 'We are able.' And he said to them, **"You might indeed drink of my cup, and be baptized with the baptism that I am baptized with: but to sit on my right hand, and on my left, is not mine to give, it will be given to them for whom it is prepared by my Father."**

155.   When the disciples heard this, they were moved with indignation against the two brothers. But Jesus called them to him, and said, **"You know that the princes of the Gentiles exercise dominion over them, and that they great exercise authority upon them. But it will not be so among you: but whoever will be great among you, let him be your minister; And who ever will be chief among you, let him be your servant: Even as the Son of man did not come to be ministered to, but to minister, and to give his life a ransom for many."** As they departed from Jericho, a great multitude followed him.

156.   Behold, two blind men sat by the way side, when they heard that Jesus was passing by, they cried out, saying, 'Have mercy on us, O Lord, *you* Son of David.' The multitude rebuked them, because they would not hold their peace: but they cried the more, saying, 'Have mercy on us, O Lord, *you* Son of David'. And Jesus stopped, and called them, and said, **"What do you wish me to do for you?"** They said to him, 'Lord, that our eyes may be opened'. So Jesus had

compassion *on them,* and touched their eyes: and immediately their eyes received sight, and they followed him.

157. When they approached Jerusalem, and came to Bethphage, near the mount of Olives, then Jesus sent two disciples, Saying to them, **"Go into the village over there, and straightway you will find an ass tied, and a colt with her: loose** *them,* **and bring** *them* **unto me. And if anyone says anything to you, tell them, The Lord has need of them; and straightway he will send them."** All this was done, that it might be fulfilled which was spoken by the prophet, saying, Tell you the daughter of Zion, Behold, your King cometh unto you, meek, and sitting upon an ass, and a colt the foal of an ass. And the disciples went, and did as Jesus commanded them, and brought the ass, and the colt, and put their clothes on them, and they set *Jesus on them*.

158. And a very great multitude spread their garments in the way; others cut down branches from the trees, and threw *them* in the way. And the multitudes that went before, and that followed, cried, saying, Hosanna to the Son of David; blessed *is* he who comes in the name of the Lord, Hosanna in the highest. And when he came into Jerusalem, all the city was moved, saying, 'Who is this?' And the multitude said, this is Jesus the prophet of Nazareth of Galilee.

159. And Jesus went to the temple of God, and cast out all those who sold and bought in the temple, and overthrew the tables of the moneychangers, and the seats of those who sold doves, and said to them, **"It is written, my house will be called the house of prayer; but you have made it a den of thieves"**. And the blind and the lame came to him in

the temple; and he healed them. And when the chief priests and scribes saw the wonderful things that he did and the children crying in the temple, and saying, 'Hosanna to the Son of David'; they were very displeased, and they said to him, do you hear what they are saying? And Jesus said to them, **"Yes, have you never read, 'Out of the mouth of babes and sucklings you will receive praise'?"**

160.   And he left them, and went out of the city into Bethany; and he lodged there. Now in the morning as he returned into the city, he grew hungry. And when he saw a fig tree in the way, he came to it, and found nothing on it but leaves, and said to it, **"Let no fruit grow on you henceforward forever"**. And presently the fig tree withered away. And when the disciples saw *it,* they marveled, saying, 'how soon the fig tree withered away'! Jesus answered and said to them, **"Verily, I say to you, if you have faith, and do not doubt, you will be able to do this that was done to the fig tree, but also if you will say to that mountain, be moved, and thrown into the sea! And it will be done. And all things, whatever you will ask in prayer, believing, you will receive."**

161.   And when he came into the temple, the chief priests and the elders of the people came to him as he was teaching, and said, By what authority do you do these things, and who gave you this authority? Jesus answered and said to them, **"I also will ask you one thing, which if you tell me, I will likewise tell you by what authority I do these things. ' The baptism of John, where was it from? From heaven or of men'?"** And they reasoned with themselves, saying, 'If we will say, from heaven; he will say

to us, why did you not then believe him'?" However, if we will say, of men, we fear the people, for they hold John as a prophet. And they answered Jesus, and said, 'We cannot tell.' And he said to them, "**Neither will I tell you by what authority I do these things.**"

162. "But what do you think of this situation? A *certain* man had two sons; and he came to the first, and said, Son, go work today in my vineyard. He answered and said, 'I will not: but afterward he repented, and went.' And he came to the second, and said likewise. And he answered and said, 'I will *go,* sir: and went not'. Which of the two did the will of *his* father?" They said to him, 'The first'. Jesus said to them, "**Verily, I say unto you, that the publicans and the harlots go into the kingdom of God before you. For John came to you in the way of righteousness and you did not believe him: but the publicans and the harlots believed him: and you, when you had seen** *it,* **did not repent afterward, so that you might believe him.**"

163. "Hear another parable. There was a certain householder, who planted a vineyard and hedged it round about and dug a winepress in it, and built a tower, and let it out to husbandmen. He then left and went into a far country. And when the time for the fruit drew near, he sent his servants to the husbandmen, so that they might receive the fruits of it. Moreover, the husbandmen took his servants, and they beat one, killed another, and stoned another.

164. Again, he sent other servants, and they did unto them likewise. Last of all, he sent his son to them, saying, 'They will respect my son.' But when the husbandmen saw the

son, they said among themselves, 'This is the heir; come, let us kill him, and let us seize his inheritance.' And they caught him, and cast *him* out of the vineyard, and killed *him.* **Therefore when the lord of the vineyard comes, what will he do unto those husbandmen?"** They said to him, He will miserably destroy those wicked men, and will let out *his* vineyard to other husbandmen, who will give him the fruits in their seasons.

165. Then Jesus said to them, **"Did you never read in the scriptures, 'The stone which the builders rejected, the same will become the head of the corner.' This is the Lords' doing, and it is marvelous in our eyes?' Therefore, I say to you, the kingdom of God will be taken from you, and given to another nation, bringing forth the fruit of that Kingdom. And whoever will fall on this stone will be broken: but whoever it falls on, it will grind him to powder."** When the chief priests and Pharisees heard his parables, they perceived that he spoke of them. However, when they sought to lay hands on him, they feared the multitude, because they believed him to be a prophet.

166. Jesus answered and spoke to them again in parables, and said, **"The kingdom of heaven is like a certain king, who made a marriage for his son, and sent his servants out to call those who were invited to the wedding, but they would not come. Again, he sent forth other servants, saying, Tell those who are invited, Behold, I have prepared my dinner: my oxen and my fattened calves have been killed, and all things are ready: come to the marriage. Nevertheless, people who were invited made light of it, and went their ways, one to his farm, another to his**

merchandise, and the others took his servants and treated *them* spitefully and killed *them*. When the king heard about it, he was angered, and he sent forth his armies, and destroyed those murderers, and burned up their city.

167. Then said he to his servants, 'The wedding is ready, but they who were invited have not come.' Therefore, go out onto the highways, and invite as many as you can find, to attend the marriage. So the servants went out onto the highways, and gathered together all as many as they could find, both bad and good: and the wedding was furnished with guests

168. And when the king came in to see the guests, he saw there a man who did not have on a wedding garment, and he said unto him, Friend, Why do you come in here without having a wedding garment? And the man was speechless. Then the king said to the servants, Bind him hand and foot, and take him away, and cast *him* into outer darkness; there will be weeping and gnashing of teeth. For many are called, but few *are* chosen.

169. Then the Pharisees went, and took counsel about how they might entangle him in *his* talk. And they sent their disciples along with the Herodians to him, saying, 'Master, we know that you are true, and teach the way of God in truth, neither do you fear any *man:* for you regard not the person of men. Therefore, tell us, what do you think, is it lawful to give tribute to Caesar, or not'?

170. However, Jesus perceived their wickedness, and said, **"Why tempt me, *you* hypocrites? Show me the tribute money."** Then they brought a penny to him. And he said to them, **"Whose image and writing is this?"** They said to him,

'Caesar's.' Then said he to them, **"Render therefore unto Caesar the things which are Caesar's; and unto God the things that are God's."** When they had heard *these words,* they marveled, and left, and went their way.

171. The same day the Sadducees came to him, (who say that there is no resurrection), and asked him, 'Master, Moses said, 'If a man dies, leaving no children, then his brother must marry the wife, and have children with her for his brother's sake. Now there were seven brothers. The first, married a wife, then he died, leaving no children, and left his wife to the first brother: Likewise for the second also, and the third, until the seventh. Finally, the woman died too.

172. Therefore, in the resurrection, whose wife will she be of the seven? Because they all had her. Jesus answered and said to them, '**You are wrong, you do not know the scriptures, or the power of God. For in the resurrection they neither marry, nor are given in marriage, but are as the angels of God in heaven. However, as to the resurrection of the dead, have you not read that which was spoken to you by God, saying, 'I am the God of Abraham, and the God of Isaac, and the God of Jacob!' God is not the God of the dead, but of the living."** When the multitude heard *this,* they were astonished at his doctrine.

173. But when the Pharisees heard that he had put the Sadducees to silence, they gathered together. Then one of them, *who was* a lawyer, asked Jesus a question, tempting him, and saying, 'Master, which *is* the greatest commandment of the law?' Jesus said to him, "**You will love**

the Lord your God with all your heart, and with all your soul, and with all your mind. This is the first and greatest commandment. The second *is* similar to the first, Love your neighbor as you do yourself. On these two commandments hang all the law and the prophets."

174. While the Pharisees gathered together, Jesus asked them, Saying, "**What do you think of Christ? Whose son is he?**" They said to him, '*The Son* of David.' He said to them, "**How then does David in spirit call him Lord, saying, The LORD said unto my Lord, sit you on my right hand, I will make your enemies your footstool? If David called him Lord, how is he his son?**" No man was able to answer him a word, and no one from that day forth dared to ask him any more *questions*.

175. Then spoke Jesus to the multitude, and to his disciples, Saying, "**The scribes and the Pharisees sit in Moses' seat: Whatever they bid you to observe, observe** *that* **and do it; but do not do their works: for they say things, and do not do them. They bind men with burdens that are heavy and grievous to be borne, and lay** *them* **on men's shoulders; but they** *themselves* **will not lift one of their fingers to help. All the works they do they do to be seen of men: they make broad their prayer boxes, and enlarge the borders of their garments, and love the uppermost rooms at feasts, and the chief seats in the synagogues, and greetings in the markets, and to be called of men, Rabbi, Rabbi. But they should not be called Rabbi: for one is your Master,** *even* **Christ, and you are all brothers and sons of God. Call no** *man* **your father upon the Earth: for only one is your Father, who is in heaven. Do not call yourselves**

masters: for only one is your Master, This is so, *even* for the Christ. He that is greatest among you will be your servant and whoever will exalt himself will be debased and he that will humble himself will be exalted.

176. But woe to you scribes and Pharisees, hypocrites! For you shut the kingdom of heaven up against men: you cannot go in yourselves, and you will not allow those who wish to enter to go in. Woe unto you scribes and Pharisees, you are hypocrites! You devour widows' houses, and make pretence of long prayer. Therefore, you will receive the greater damnation. Woe unto you, you scribes and Pharisees, you hypocrites! For you encompass sea and land to make one convert, but when he is converted, you make him twice more a child of hell than yourselves.

177. Woe unto you, *you* blind guides, who say, Whoever will swear by the temple, it is nothing; but who ever will swear by the gold of the temple, he is a debtor to the temple! *You* fools and blind men: for what is greater, the gold, or the temple that sanctifies the gold? Moreover, whoever swears by the altar, it is nothing; but whoever swears by the gift that is upon it, he is guilty. *You* fools and blind men: for what *is* greater, the gift, or the altar that sanctifies the gift?

178. Therefore, whoever swear by the altar, swears by it and by all things on it. Whoever swears by the temple, swears on it, and by him that dwells therein. And he that will swear by heaven, swears by the throne of God, and by he who sits on it.

179. Woe unto you, scribes and Pharisees, you malignant hypocrites! For you pay tithe of mint and anise and cumin, but have forgotten the weightier *matters* of the law, judgment, mercy, and faith: these are the things you ought to have done, and have left the other things undone. *You* blind guides, who strain at a gnat, and swallow a camel. Woe to you, you scribes and Pharisees. Hypocrites! For you make clean the outside of the cup and the bowl, but inside they are full of extortion and excess. *You* blind Pharisees, cleanse first that *which is* within the cup and bowl so that the outside of them may be clean too.

180. Woe unto you, scribes and Pharisees, hypocrites! For you are like whitened sepulchers, which appear beautiful outward indeed, but, in truth, are full of dead *men's* bones, and uncleanness. Even so, you outwardly appear righteous to men, but within you are full of hypocrisy and iniquity.

181. Woe unto you, scribes and Pharisees, hypocrites! Because you build the tombs of the prophets, and garnish the sepulchers of the righteous, and you say, if we had been there in the days of our fathers, we would not have partaken in the blood of the prophets. Therefore, you are witnesses to your own selves, as you are the children of those who killed the prophets. Fill yourself up with the measure of your fathers. *You* serpents, *you* generation of vipers, how can you escape the damnation of hell?

182. Wherefore, behold, I send to you prophets, and wise men, and scribes: and *some* of them you will kill and crucify; and *some* of them will you vilify in your synagogues, and persecute *them* from city to city: So that

all the righteous bloodshed upon the earth may come upon you.

183. From the blood of righteous Abel to the blood of Zacharias son of Barachias who you slew between the temple and the altar. Verily, I say unto you, all these things will come upon this generation. O, Jerusalem, Jerusalem, *you* who kill the prophets, and stone those who are sent to you. How often would I have gathered your children together, even as a hen gathers her chickens under *her* wings, and you would not repent! Behold, your house will be left desolate. For I say unto you, you will not see me again, till you will say, blessed *is* he that cometh in the name of the Lord."

184. Then Jesus went out, and departed from the temple: and his disciples came to *him* to show him the buildings of the temple. And Jesus said to them, **"Do you not see all these things? Verily, I say unto you, there will not be left one stone upon another that will not be thrown down."**

185. And as he sat upon the Mount of Olives, the disciples came to him privately, saying, 'Tell us, when these things will happen? And what will be the sign of your coming, and of the end of the world'? And Jesus answered and said to them, **"Take heed so that no man will deceive you. For many will come in my name, saying, I am Christ; and they will deceive many. And you will hear of wars and rumors of wars: but do not be troubled: for all *these things* must come to pass, but the end is not yet. For nation will rise against nation, and kingdom against kingdom: and there will be famines, and pestilences, and earthquakes, in diverse places.**

186. All these *are* the beginning of sorrows. Then will they deliver you up to be afflicted, and they will kill you, and you will be hated by all nations for my name's sake. Then, many will be offended, and they will betray one another, and will hate one another.

187. Many false prophets will rise, and they will deceive many. And because iniquity will abound, the love of many will grow cold. However, he who will endure to the end will be saved. And this gospel of the kingdom will be preached in all the world as a witness to all nations; and then will the end come. Therefore, then you will see the abomination of desolation, spoken of by Daniel the prophet, standing in a holy place.

188. Then let them who are in Judaea flee into the mountains: Let him who is on the housetop not come down to take anything out of his house: Neither let him who is in the field return back to take his clothes. And woe unto them that are with child and to them that give suck in those days! But pray you that your flight should not happen in the winter, or on the Sabbath day: For there will be great tribulation, such as was not seen since the beginning of the world to this time, no, or ever will be.

189. In addition, if it were not that those days of tribulation were shortened, no flesh would be saved: it is only for the sake of the chosen that those days of trouble will be shortened.

190. Then if any man will say to you, 'Lo, here *is* Christ, or he is there; *Do* not believe it.' For there will arise false Christs, and false prophets, and they will show great signs and wonders; so much so, that, if *it were* possible, they

would deceive even the very elect. Behold, I have told you before. Therefore, if they will say to you, Behold, *he is* in the desert; do not go there: behold, he is in the secret chambers; do not believe it. For as the lightning comes out of the east, and shines even unto the west, so will the coming of the Son of man be. For wherever the carcass is, the vultures will be gathered there also.

191. Immediately after the tribulation of those days, the sun will be darkened, the moon will not give her light, the stars will fall from heaven, and the powers of the heavens will be shaken. Then the sign of the Son of man in heaven will appear, and all the tribes of the earth will mourn, and they will see the Son of man coming in the clouds of heaven with power and great glory.

192. And he will send his angels with a great sound of a trumpet, and they will gather together his elect from the four winds, from one end of heaven to the other.

193. Now learn the parable of the fig tree; When its branches are young and tender, and put forth leaves, you know that summer is near: So likewise, when you see all these signs, know that the time is near, *even* at the door. Verily, I say unto you, this generation will not pass, until all these things are fulfilled. Heaven and earth will pass away, but my words will not pass.

194. But, about the day and hour of that coming, no *man* knows, no, not even the angels of heaven, only our Father knows. Just as the days of Noah *were,* so will the coming of the Son of man be also. For as in the days that were before the flood they were eating and drinking, marrying and giving in marriage, until the day that Noah entered

into the ark, they knew nothing until the flood came, and took them all away. So too will the coming of the Son of man be. There will two be in the field, one will be taken, and the other left. Two women will be grinding at the mill; one will be taken, and the other left.

195.   Therefore, watch! For you do not know what hour your Lord will come. But know this, that if the good man of the house had known in what hour the thief would come, he would have watched, and would not have allowed his house to be destroyed. Therefore, be ready!

196.   For in that hour that you do not think that the Son of man comes, that is when he will come. Who then is a faithful and wise servant, who his lord has made ruler over his household, and given them food in due season? Blessed *is* that servant, who, when his lord comes come will find still faithful. Verily, I say unto you, that he will make him ruler over all his goods. However, if that evil servant will hear in his ear, 'My lord is not coming.' And begins to hit his fellow servants, and to eat and drink with the lushes. The lord of that servant will come in a day when the servant is not looking for him, and at a time that he is not aware of, and will cut him down, and give him his portion with the hypocrites, and there will be weeping and gnashing of teeth.

197.   Then the kingdom of heaven is like the ten virgins, who took their lamps, and went forth to meet the bridegroom. Five of them were wise, and five were foolish. Those who were foolish took their lamps, and took no oil with them: But the wise took oil in their vessels with their lamps. While the bridegroom tarried, they all slumbered

and slept. And at midnight there was a cry made, Behold, the bridegroom comes, go out to meet him.

198. Then all those virgins arose, and trimmed their lamps. The foolish ones said to the wise, 'Give us some of your oil; our lamps have gone out.' But the wise ones answered, saying, *'No;* unless there will not be enough for all of us.' Go to those who sell oil, and buy some for yourselves. And while they went to buy, the bridegroom came; and the five who were ready went in with him to the marriage: and the door was shut. Afterward the other virgins came, saying, 'Lord! Lord! Open the door for us.' But the lord answered and said, 'Verily, I say unto you, I do not know you.' Therefore, watch, for you will not know either the day or the hour when the Son of man will come.

199. For *the kingdom of heaven is* like a man travelling into a far country, *who* called together his servants and delivered his fortune to them. To one he gave five talents, to another two, and to another one; to each man according to his ability; and straightway went on his journey. Then the one that had received the five talents went and traded with them, and made five more talents. In addition, the one who *received* two talents gained another two. But the one who received one talent dug in the earth, and hid his lord's money. After a long time the lord of those servants returned, and reckoned with them.

200. The servant that received five talents came and brought other five talents, saying, Lord, you gave me five talents: behold, I have earned five more talents. His lord said unto him, Well done, *you* are a good and faithful servant: you have been faithful over a few things, I will

make you ruler over many things: enter you into the joy of your lord. The one who received two talents came and said, Lord, you gave me two talents: behold, I have earned two other talents beside them. His lord said unto him, well done, you are a good and faithful servant also; you have been faithful over a few things, I will make you ruler over many things: enter you into the joy of your lord.

201. Then the one that received one talent came and said, Lord, I knew you that you are an hard man, reaping where you have not sown, and gathering where you have not sown: And I was afraid, and I went and hid your talent in the earth: So, *here* I return that which is yours.

202. The lord answered and said to him, *You* are a wicked and slothful servant, you knew that I reaped where I did not sow, and gathered where I have not sown: You should have given my money to the exchangers, and *then* when I returned, I would have received my own with interest.

203. Therefore, I will take the one talent from him, and give it to him who has ten talents. For unto he who has been diligent, more will be given and he will have abundance: but from him that has not been wise, I will take away even that which he has left. And I will cast him, into the outer darkness and there will be weeping and gnashing of teeth.

204. When the Son of man will come in his glory, and all the holy angels with him, then he will sit upon the throne of his glory. And before him all nations will be gathered and he will separate them one from another, as a shepherd divides *his* sheep from the goats: And he will set the sheep on his right hand, and the goats on the left. Then the king will say to those on his right hand, Come, you are blessed

by my Father, and will inherit the kingdom prepared for you from the foundation of the world.

205. For I was hungry, and you gave me food: I was thirsty, and you gave me drink: I was a stranger, and you took me in: I was naked, and you clothed me: I was sick, and you watched over me: I was in prison, and you came to visit me. Then the righteous will answer him, saying, Lord, when we saw you and you were hungry, we fed *you,* and when you were thirsty, we gave *you* drink. When saw we you were a stranger we took *you* in. and when we found you naked, and we clothed *you?* When we saw you were sick, or in prison, we came to visit you.

206. And the King will answer and say unto them, Verily I say to you, Inasmuch as you have done these things for one of the least of these my brothers, you have done it for me. Then he will say to them on the left hand, Depart from me you cursed ones, into the everlasting fire, prepared by the devil and his angels. For I when was hungry, and you gave me no meat: when I was thirsty, and you gave me nothing to drink: I was a stranger, and you did not take me in. When I was naked, you gave me no clothes. When I was sick, and in prison, and you did not visit me.

207. Then will they also answer to him, saying, Lord, when saw we you were hungry, thirsty, or a stranger, or naked, or sick, or in prison, we did not minister unto you? Then the Lord will he answer them, saying, Verily, I say to you, Inasmuch as you did *not do these things* for one of the least of these, you did *not do it for me*. And those evil ones will go away into everlasting punishment, but the righteous ones will go on to eternal life."

208. And it came to pass, when Jesus had finished all these sayings, he said unto his disciples, **"You know that in two days *the feast of* the Passover will come, and the Son of man will be betrayed and crucified".**

209. Then the chief priests, and the scribes, and the elders of the people assembled at the palace of the high priest, who was called Caiaphas. They consulted among themselves that they might take Jesus by subterfuge, and kill *him*. But they said, not on the feast *day,* there might be an uproar among the people.

210. Now when Jesus was in Bethany, in the house of Simon the leper, a woman came to him there who had an alabaster box of very precious ointment, and who poured it on his head, as he sat *eating.* However, when his disciples saw *it,* they were indignant, saying, 'To what purpose *is* this waste? This ointment might have been sold and given to the poor.' When Jesus heard this, he said to them, **"Why do you trouble the woman? She has done something of value for me. The poor will always be with you; but you will not have me always. This woman, by pouring ointment on my body, has prepared me for my burial. Verily, I say unto you, Wherever this gospel will be preached in the whole world, all will remember what this woman has done, it will be a memorial to her."**

211. Then one of the twelve, called Judas Iscariot, went to the chief priests, and said to them, what will you give me if I will deliver Jesus to you? And they agreed with him on thirty pieces of silver, and from that time, he sought an opportunity to betray him.

212. On the first *day* of the *feast of* unleavened bread, the disciples came to Jesus, saying to him, where do you want us to go to prepare for Passover? He said, **"Go into the city to a householder, and say unto him, The Master said, 'My time is at hand; I will keep the Passover at your house with my disciples.'"** The disciples did as Jesus had appointed them; and they made ready the Passover. Now when the event came, he sat down with the twelve. As they ate, he said, **"Verily, I say to you, one of you will betray me."**

213. They were exceeding sorrowful, and began every one of them to say to him, Lord, is it I? And he answered and said, **"He that dips *his* hand with me in the dish, the same will betray me. The Son of man proceeds as it is written for him: but woe unto that man by whom the Son of man is betrayed! It would have been better if that man had never been born."** Then Judas, who betrayed him, answered and said, 'Master, is it I'? He said to him, **"You have said it."**

214. AS they were eating, Jesus took bread, and blessed *it*, and broke *it*, and gave *it* to the disciples, and said, **"Take, eat; this is my body".** He took up a cup of win, and gave thanks, and gave *it* to them, saying, **"Drink all of it, for this is my blood of the new testament, which is shed for many for the remission of sins. But I say to you, I will not drink again of this fruit of the vine, until that day when I drink it new with you in my Father's kingdom."**

215. After they sang a hymn, they went out onto the Mount of Olives. Then said Jesus to them, **"All of you will be offended because of me this night: for it is written, 'I will smite the shepherd, and the sheep of the flock will be scattered abroad.' But after I have risen again, I will go**

before you into Galilee." Peter replied and said to him, 'Yes, some might be offended because of you, *but* I will never be offended'. Jesus said to him**, "Verily' I say to you, that this night, before the cock crows, you will deny me thrice."** Peter said to him, 'No! I will die with you, No! I will not deny you'. All the other disciples said Likewise.

216. Then Jesus came with them to a place called Gethsemane, and said to the disciples**, "Sit here, while I go and pray over there".** And he took Peter with him and the two sons of Zebedee, and began to be sorrowful and very heavy. Then said he to them, **"My soul is exceedingly sorrowful, even unto death: wait here, and watch with me."** Then he went a little farther, and fell on his face, and prayed, saying, **"O my Father, if it be possible, let this cup pass from me,** Then he recanted, saying", **But not as I will, but as you** *will".*

217. Later, he came back to the disciples, and found them asleep, and said to Peter, **"What! Could you not watch with me one hour? Watch and pray that you do not enter into temptation."** Adding, **"The spirit indeed** *is* **willing, but the flesh** *is* **weak".** He went away again a second time, and prayed, saying, **"O, my Father, if this cup may not pass away from me, I will drink it, and your will be done."** And he came and found them asleep again, for their eyes were heavy. And he left them, and went away again, and prayed the third time, saying the same words. Then he returned to his disciples, and said to them, **"Sleep on now, and take** *your* **rest: behold, the hour is at hand, and the Son of man will be betrayed into the hands of sinners. Rise, let us be going: behold, he is at hand who has betrayed me."**

218. And while he thus spoke, lo, Judas, one of the twelve, came, and with him a great multitude with swords and staves, sent by the chief priests and elders of the people. Now Judas gave them a sign, saying, 'Whomever I kiss, that is he: hold him fast'. He walked right up to Jesus, and said, 'Hail, master'; and kissed him. And Jesus said to him, "My **Friend, where have been?"**

219. Then they came and laid hands on Jesus, and took him. And, behold, one of those who was with Jesus reached down, drew his sword, and struck a servant of the high priest's and cut off his ear. Then said Jesus to the man, **"Put away your sword. For all who take up the sword will perish by the sword. Do you not believe that I can pray to my Father and he will presently give me more than twelve legions of angels? But how then will the scriptures be fulfilled if that happened, so thus it must be?"**

220. At that same time, Jesus said to the multitudes who accosted him, **"Have you come, as against a thief, with swords and staves to take me? I sat daily with you teaching in the temple, and you laid no hold on me. All this was done, so that the scriptures of the prophets could be fulfilled."** Then all the disciples forsook him, and fled.

221. They that had laid hold on Jesus led *him* away to Caiaphas the high priest, where the scribes and the elders had assembled. But Peter followed him, from a distance, to the high priest's palace, and went in and sat with the servants to see what would happen.

222. Now the chief priests, and elders, and all the council, sought witnesses against Jesus, to put him to death, but they found none: yes, many false witnesses came, *but* found

they had no valid complaint. At last there came two false witnesses, who said, 'This fellow, Jesus, said, 'I am able to destroy the temple of God, and to rebuild it in three days'.

223. Upon which the high priest arose, and said to Jesus, do you have an answer to anything that these witness say against you? But Jesus held his peace, and the high priest answered and said to him, I charge you, by the living God, that you tell us whether you are the Christ, the Son of God. Jesus said to him, "**You have spoken: nevertheless I say unto you, Hereafter will you see the Son of man sitting on the right hand of power, and coming in the clouds of heaven."**

224. Then the high priest tore Jesus' clothes, saying, 'He has spoken blasphemy, what further need do we have for witnesses? Behold, now you have heard his blasphemy. What do you think?' The crowd answered and said, 'He is guilty of death. Then they spit in his face, and buffeted him; and others hit *him* with the palms of their hands, Saying, 'Tell us, Jesus the Christ, who was it who hit you'?

225. Now as Peter sat in the palace: and a girl came before him, saying, 'You were with Jesus of Galilee too. However, he denied it before *them* all, saying, 'I don't know what you're talking about'. And when he went out to the porch, another *young woman* saw him, and said to those who were there, 'This *fellow* was with that Jesus of Nazareth'. Again, he denied it with an oath, 'I do not know the man'.

226. After a while, those who stood around came to *him* and said to Peter, 'Surely you also are *one* of them; for your accent betrays you'. Then he began to curse and to swear, *saying,* 'I do not know the man!' Immediately the cock

crowed. With great sorrow, Peter remembered the word of Jesus, who had told him, "**Before the cock will crow, you will deny me thrice."** Then he went out, and wept bitterly.

227. When the morning came, all the chief priests and elders of the people took counsel against Jesus to put him to death: And when they had bound him, they led *him* away, and delivered him to Pontius Pilate the governor.

228. When Judas, who had betrayed him, saw that he was to be condemned to death, repented, and returned the thirty pieces of silver to the chief priests and elders, Saying, 'I have sinned in that I have betrayed innocent blood.' And they said, 'What *is that* to us?' That is your problem. And he cast down the pieces of silver in the temple, and departed, and went and hung himself.

229. And the chief priests took the silver pieces, and said, 'It is not lawful to return them to the treasury, because it is the price of blood.' And they took counsel, and bought the potter's field with them, to bury strangers in. Where after that field was called, the field of blood, unto this day.

230. Then it was fulfilled, that which was spoken of by Jeremy the prophet, saying, 'And they took the thirty pieces of silver, the price of him that was valued, whom they of the children of Israel did value; And paid for the potter's field, as the Lord appointed.' And Jesus stood before the governor: and the governor asked him, saying, Are you the King of the Jews? And Jesus answered nothing.

231. Then Pilate said to him, 'Do you not hear how many things they have witnessed against you'? Moreover, Jesus refused to answer, insomuch that the governor marveled greatly. Now at *that* feast, the governor was accustomed to

release to the people a prisoner, that the wanted released. And they had then a notable prisoner, called Barabbas. Therefore, when they were gathered together, Pilate said to them, 'who do you want for me to release to you'? Barabbas or Jesus who is called Christ? Because he knew that they had delivered Jesus to him from envy.

232. When he sat down on the judgment seat, his wife came to him, saying, Have nothing to do with that just man: for I have suffered many things this day in a dream because of him. However, the chief priests and elders persuaded the multitude that they should ask for Barabbas, and destroy Jesus. The governor answered and said to them, 'Which of the two do you wish that I release to you'? They said, 'Barabbas'. Pilate said to them, 'What will I do then with Jesus who is called Christ?' *They* all said to him, 'Let him be crucified.' But they cried all out the more, saying, 'Let him be crucified!'".

233. When Pilate saw that he could not change crowd's mind, and that more tumult was made, he took water, and washed *his* hands before the multitude, saying, 'I am innocent of the blood of this just person: It will be on you'. Then the multitude answered, 'Yes, kill him.'

234. Then he released Barabbas to them: and when he had scourged Jesus, he delivered *him* to be crucified. Then the soldiers of the governor took Jesus into the common hall, and gathered unto him the whole band *of soldiers.* They stripped him, and put a scarlet robe on him.

235. After they fashioned a crown of thorns, they put *it* upon his head, and a reed in his right hand: and they bowed at the knee before him, and mocked him, saying, 'Hail, King of

the Jews'! They spit on him, and took the reeds and hit him on the head. After that they mocked him, they took the robe off of him, and put his own clothes back on him, and led him away to crucify *him.* As they came out, they found a man of Cyrene, Simon by name, and they compelled him to bear the cross.

236. When they came to the place called Golgotha, that is to say, 'the place of the skull', they gave him vinegar to drink mingled with gall: and when he had taste*d it* he would not drink. Then they crucified him, and paraded his garments, casting lots: that it might be fulfilled which was spoken by the prophet. They paraded his garments among them, and they laid down his clothes and threw dice on them.

237. They sat down as in a show, and they watched him there; and set up over his head his accusation written thus, 'THIS IS JESUS THE KING OF THE JEWS.' There were also two thieves crucified along with him, one on the right hand, and another on the left.

238. And crowd that passed by reviled him, wagging their heads, saying, 'You who destroyed the temple, and rebuilt *it* in three days, save yourself if you are the Son of God, come down from the cross'. Likewise, the chief priests mocked him. The scribes and elders, said, 'He saved others; but himself he cannot save. If he is the King of Israel, let him come down from the cross, and we will believe him. He trusted in God; let him deliver him now', if he will have him: for he said, 'I am the Son of God'. The thieves also, who were crucified with him, cast the same aspersions in his face.

239. Now from the sixth hour there was darkness over all the land unto the ninth hour. In the ninth hour, Jesus cried with a loud voice, saying, **"Eli, Eli, lama sabachthani?"** that is to say**, "My God, my God, why have you forsaken me?"** Some of them that stood there, when they heard *that,* said, 'This *man* calls for Elias.' And straightway one of them ran, took a sponge, filled it with vinegar, put *it* on a reed, and gave it to him to drink. The rest of them said, 'Let him be, let us see whether Elias will come to save him'.

240. Jesus, when he cried again, cried with a loud voice, and yielded up the ghost.

The Words of Jesus According to the Gospel of St. Mark

1. After John the Baptist was put in prison, Jesus came into Galilee, preaching the gospel of the kingdom of God, and saying, "**The time is fulfilled, and the kingdom of God is at hand: repent you, and believe the gospel.**" Now as he walked by the Sea of Galilee, he saw Simon and Andrew his brother casting a net into the sea: for they were fishermen. And Jesus said to them, "**Follow me, and I will make you fishers of men**". And straightway they forsook their nets, and followed him. And when he had gone a little farther thence, he saw James the *son* of Zebedee, and John his brother, who also were in a ship mending their nets. Straightway he called them, and they left their father Zebedee in the ship with the hired servants, and went after him.

2. They went into Capernaum; and straightway on the Sabbath day, he entered into the synagogue, and taught. And they who heard him were astonished at his doctrines: for he taught them as one that had authority, and not as the scribes. There was in their synagogue a man with an unclean spirit; and the unclean spirit cried out, Saying, 'Let *us* alone; what have we to do with you, you Jesus of Nazareth? Are you come to destroy us? I know you who you are, the Holy One of God'. And Jesus rebuked him, saying, "**Hold your peace, and come out of him**". Then the unclean spirit shook the man, and cried with a loud voice, he came out of him. They were all amazed, insomuch that they questioned among themselves, saying, what do these things

mean? What new doctrine *is* this? He commanded even the unclean spirits with authority, and they obey him.
3. Immediately his fame spread abroad throughout the entire region round about Galilee. And forthwith, when they came out of the synagogue, they entered into the house of Simon and Andrew, with James and John. But Simon's wife's mother lay sick of a fever and they told Jesus about her. And he came and took her by the hand, and lifted her up; and immediately the fever left her, and she ministered to them.
4. And in the evening, when the sun set, they brought to him all that were diseased, and those who were possessed with devils. And all the city gathered together at the door. And he healed many that were sick of diverse diseases, and cast out many devils; and did not allow the devils to speak, because they knew him.
5. The next morning, rising up a great while before daybreak, he went out and departed to a solitary place, and prayed there. And Simon and those who were with him followed after him. And when they had found him, they said to him, 'All *men* seek you', and He said to them, **"Let us go into the next towns so that I may preach there also: for there I will come forth."**
6. And he preached in their synagogues throughout all Galilee, and cast out devils. And came a leper to him there, pleading with him, and kneeling down to him, and saying to him, 'If you will it, you can make me clean'. And Jesus, moved with compassion, put forth *his* hand, and touched him, and said unto him, **"I will it; be clean!"** And as soon as

he had spoken, immediately the leprosy departed from him, and he was cleansed.

7. And Jesus cautioned him, and forthwith sent him away; and said unto him, "**See that you say nothing to any man: but go your way, show yourself to the priest, and offer alms for your cleansing and those things which Moses commanded, for a testimony.**" Nevertheless, he went out, and began to speak of *it* everywhere, and to spread the matter openly, so much so that Jesus could not openly enter into the city anymore. He had to stay outside in a desert place, but they still came to him from every quarter.

8. Again, he entered into Capernaum, after *some* days; and it was noised about that he was in the house. Straightway many gathered, so many that there was no room to receive *them,* no, not so much as even around the door: and he preached the word to them. And they came to him, bringing one sick of the palsy, who was borne by four people. And when they could not come near to him for the press, they uncovered the roof where he was: and when they had broken *it* up, they let down the bed where the man sick of the palsy lay.

9. When Jesus saw their faith, he said to the one sick of the palsy, "**Son, your sins are forgiven you.**" However, there were certain of the scribes sitting there, and reasoning in their hearts, 'Why does this *man* speak such blasphemies'? who can forgive sins except God only'? And immediately when Jesus perceived in his spirit that they had so reasoned within themselves, he said to them, "**Why do you reason these things in your hearts? Whether is it easier to say to the sick of the palsy, '*Your* sins are forgiven you;' or**

to say, 'Arise, and take up your bed, and walk?' **But that you may know that the Son of man hath power on earth to forgive sins, (speaking to the man sick of the palsy,) I say to you, Arise, and take up your bed, and go your way to your house."**

10. Immediately he arose, took up his bed, and went forth before them all; so much that they were all amazed and they glorified God, saying, 'We have never seen anything like this before. And he went forth again to the sea side; and all the multitude resorted to him, and he taught them. And as he passed by, he saw Levi the *son* of Alphaeus sitting at the receipt of custom, and said to him, "**Follow me**!" And he arose and followed him.

11. And it came to pass, that, as Jesus sat at eating in Levi's house, many publicans and sinners sat also together with Jesus and his disciples: for there were many, and they followed him. And when the scribes and Pharisees saw him eat with publicans and sinners, they said to his disciples, 'How is it that he eats and drinks with publicans and sinners?' When Jesus heard *it,* he said to them, "**They that are whole have no need of the physician, but they that are sick: I came not to call the righteous, but sinners to repentance."**

12. Because the disciples of John the Baptist and the Pharisees were used to fasting, they came and said to Jesus, Why do the disciples of John and of the Pharisees fast, but your disciples do not fast? And Jesus said to them**, "Can the children of the bride chamber fast, while the bridegroom is with them? As long as they have the bridegroom with them, they cannot fast. However, the days will come,**

when the bridegroom will be taken away from them, then they will fast.

13. No man sews a piece of new cloth onto an old garment: else the new piece that fills up the hole takes away from the old cloth, and the rip is made worse. Also, no man puts new wine into old bottles: else, the new wine will crack the weak old bottles, and the wine will be spilled, and the bottles will be marred. New wine must be put into new bottles."

14. And it came to pass, that as he went through the cornfields on the Sabbath day; and his disciples began, as they went, to pluck the ears of corn. And the Pharisees said to him, 'Behold, why do they do on the Sabbath day that which is not lawful'? Jesus stopped and said to them, "**Have you never read what David did, when he had need, and was hungry, along with those that were with him? How he went into the house of God in the days of Abiathar, the high priest, and ate the showbread, which is not lawful to eat except for the priests, and gave it to those who were with him also?** And he said to the Pharisees, "**The Sabbath was made for man, and not man for the Sabbath: Therefore, the sons of man are also Lords of the Sabbath.**"

15. And he entered again into the synagogue; and there was a man there who had a withered hand. And they watched him, to see if Jesus would heal him on the Sabbath day, so that they might accuse him. And he said to the man who had the withered hand, "**Stand up**". And he said to them, "**Is it lawful to do good on the Sabbath days, or to do evil? To save life, or to kill?**"

16. However, they held their peace. And when he had looked round about at them with anger, being saddened by the hardness of their hearts, he said to the afflicted man, **"Stretch forth your hand"**. Then the scribes who came down from Jerusalem said, 'He does the work of Beelzebub, and by the power of the prince of the devils he cast out devils.' And Jesus called them *to him,* and said to them in parables, **"How can Satan cast out Satan? If a kingdom is divided against itself, that kingdom cannot stand. If a house is divided against itself, that house cannot stand. If Satan rises up against himself, and is divided, he cannot stand, but will be destroyed.**
17. **No man can enter into a strong man's house, and spoil his goods, except he first bind the strong man; after that, he can ransack his house. Verily, I say to you, All sins will be forgiven for the sons of men, and the blasphemies whereby they blaspheme against other men: But he that will blasphemes against the Holy Ghost will never have forgiveness, but is in danger of eternal damnation: Because he has an unclean spirit."**
18. Then there came his brothers and his mother, standing outside, calling for him. And the multitude that sat about him, said to him, 'Behold, your mother and your brothers are outside and are asking for you'. And he answered them, saying, **"Who is my mother, or my brothers?"** and he looked round about on those who sat about him, and said, **"Behold my mother and my brothers! For whoever will do the will of God, is the same as my brother, my sister, and my mother."**

19. And he began to teach by the seaside again, and there a great multitude gathered to see him, so many that he entered onto a ship, and sat in the boat; and the whole multitude was by the sea on the land. And he taught them many things in parables, and spoke to them about his doctrine, **"Listen; Behold, there once was a farmer who went out to sow his seeds: And it came to pass, as he sowed, some fell by the way side, and the fowls of the air came and devoured them up. In addition, some fell on stony ground, where there was not much soil; and immediately it sprang up, because it had no depth of earth: But when the sun was up, it was scorched; and because it had no root, it withered away.**
20. **Some seeds fell among thorns, and the thorns grew up, and choked them, and they yielded no fruit. And other seeds fell on good ground, and yielded fruit that sprang up and increased; and brought forth, some thirty, and some sixty, and some an hundred.** He continued, **"He that hath ears to hear, let him hear!"**
21. Later, when he was alone, with the twelve, they asked of him about the parable. He said to them, **"to you it is given to know the mystery of the kingdom of God: but to them that are without this knowledge, all these *things* are done in parables. That seeing they may see, and not perceive; and hearing they may hear, and not understand, it is told as an expedient means so that if at any time they should be converted, *their* sins would be forgiven them."** And he said to them, **"Don't you understand this parable? Then how will you know any of the parables?"**

22. Then Jesus explained the parable to the disciples in detail. "The Word is the seed. The wayside is those who seek, wherein the word is sown.
23. The seeds that are eaten by the fowl represent those who when they hear the word, Satan immediately comes, and takes away the word that was sown in their hearts.
24. Likewise, there are those in which the seeds are sown on stony ground; who, when they have heard the word, immediately receive it with gladness, but they have no root in themselves, and so persevere only for a time afterward. But when affliction or persecution arises for the word's sake, immediately they become distracted and turn from the word to other things
25. And there are those who can be liken with the seeds are sown among thorns; such of these that hear the word, but because of the cares of this world, and the deceitfulness of riches, and the lusts of other things entering that enter into them, choke on the word, and it becomes unfruitful.
26. Then there are those seeds that are sown on good ground; such are people who hear the word, and receive *it,* and bring forth fruit, some thirtyfold, some sixty, and some an hundred."
27. And he said to them, "**Is a candle meant to be put under a bushel, or under a bed and not set on a candlestick?** For there is nothing hid, which will not be made manifest; neither was anything kept secret, except that it should become known. If any man has ears to hear, let him hear."

28. And he said to them, "**Take heed what you hear: with whatever measure you deserve, it will be measured out to you: and to you that hear will more be given. For he that has, more will be given: and he that has not, from him will be taken even that which he has.**" In addition, he said, **"So it is in the kingdom of God, as if a man should cast seeds into the ground; and he would sleep, and rise night and day, and the seed would spring and grow up and he knows not how. For the earth brings forth fruit of herself. First the blade, then the ear, after that the full corn in the ear appears. But when the fruit is ripe, immediately the farmer picks up the sickle, because the time of harvest has come."**
29. And he said, **"Unto what will we liken the kingdom of God? On the other hand, with what will we compare it?** *It is* **like a grain of mustard seed, which, when it is planted in the earth, is smaller than all the other seeds of the earth: But when it is sown, it grows up, and becomes greater than all herbs, and shoots out great branches; so that the fowls of the air may lodge under the shadow of it."**
30. And with many such parables he spoke the word to the multitudes, as they were able to hear *it*. He only spoke to the multitudes with parables. When Jesus and his disciples were alone, he expounded all things to them.
31. And the same day, when the evening came, he said to them**, "Let us pass over to the other side".** And when they had sent away the multitude, they sought him even as he was in the ship. And there were with them other little ships. Moreover, there arose a great storm of wind, and

the waves beat into the ship, so that it was now full of water.

32. Jesus was in the back part of the ship, asleep on a pillow: and they woke him, and said to him, 'Master, Do you not care that we might perish'? He arose, and rebuked the wind, and spoke to the Sea**, "Peace! Be still."** And the wind ceased, and there was a great calm. And he said to them." **Why are you so fearful? How is it that you have no faith?"** And they feared exceedingly, and said one to another, 'What manner of man is this, that even the wind and the sea obey him'?

33. They came over unto the other side of the sea, into the country of the Gadarenes. And when he left the ship, immediately a man there came out of the tombs with an unclean spirit, who lived among the tombs and no man could bind him, no, not even with chains. Because he had been often bound with fetters and chains, and the chains had been plucked asunder by him, and the fetters broken in pieces. No *man* could tame him. And always, night and day, he was in the mountains, and in the tombs, crying, and cutting himself with stones.

34. However, when he saw Jesus afar off, he ran and worshipped him, and cried with a loud voice, and said, 'what have I to do with you, Jesus, *you* Son of the most high God?' I beg you, by God, that you not torment me.' Jesus replied to him, **"Come out of the man, *you* unclean spirit."** And the spirit came out and Jesus asked him, **"What *is* your name?"** And the unclean spirits begged him that he would not send them away out of the country.

35. Now there was there, nearby, on the mountain, a great herd of swine feeding. All the devils pleaded with him, saying, 'Send us to the swine, that we may enter into them.' Forthwith Jesus gave them leave. Then the unclean spirits went out, and entered into the swine: and the herd ran violently down a steep place into the sea, (there were about two thousand) and were drowned in the sea.
36. And they that herded the swine fled and told *it* in the city, and in the country. And the country folk went out to see what had happened. They came to Jesus, and saw the man who was possessed by the devil, sitting with the legion, clothed, and in his right mind and the country people were afraid. And they spoke with the witnesses who saw what happened to the man that was possessed of the devil, and *about* the pigs.
37. The countrymen, being afraid, asked Jesus to leave their coasts. And when Jesus came to the ship, the man who had been possessed with the devil asked that he might come too. However, Jesus did not allow him to come and said to him, "**Go home to your friends, and tell them what great things the Lord has done for you, and how he has had compassion on you.**"
38. The man departed, and began to speak of Jesus' teachings in Decapolis about the great things Jesus had done for him: and all *men* did marvel. And when Jesus passed over again by ship to the other side, many people gathered around him. He was near the sea when, behold, there came one of the rulers of the synagogue, Jairus by name; and when he saw Jesus, he fell at his feet, and pleaded him greatly, saying, 'My little daughter lies at the point of death. I pray

for you to come and lay your hands on her, so that she may be healed and that she will live.' And Jesus went with him; and many people followed him, and thronged him.

39. And a certain woman, who had an issue of blood for twelve years, who had suffered many things from many physicians, who had spent all that she had, and had not gotten better but worse. When she had heard of Jesus, she came behind, in the press, and touched his garment. For she thought to herself, if I may touch but his clothes, I will be whole. And straightway the fountain of her blood was dried up; and she felt in *her* body that she was healed of that plague. And Jesus, immediately knowing in himself that virtue had gone out of him, turned him about in the press of the crowd, and said, "**Who touched my clothes?**" And his disciples said to him, 'You see the multitude thronging you, and you say**, "Who touched me?"**' And he looked round about to see who had done this thing. The woman fearing and trembling, knowing what was done in her, came and fell down before him, and told him all the truth. He said to her, "**Daughter, your faith hath made you whole; go in peace, and be cured of your plague."**

40. While he thus spoke, there came the ruler of the synagogue's *house with a man, who* said, 'Your daughter is dead: why trouble the Master any further'? As soon as Jesus heard these words that were spoken, he said to the ruler of the synagogue, **"Be not afraid, only believe".** And he allowed no one to follow him, except Peter, and James, and John the brother of James.

41. And he went to the house of the ruler of the synagogue, and saw the tumult, and those who wept and wailed

greatly. When he came in, he said unto them, "**Why make you this ado, and weep? The girl is not dead, she is asleep.**" They laughed at Jesus with scorn. But when he had put them all out, he took the father and the mother of the child, and they who were with them, and entered into where the damsel was lying, and he took the girl by the hand, and said to her, "**Talitha cumi**"; which is, being interpreted, "**Damsel, I say unto you, arise.**" And straightway the girl arose, and walked; she was twelve years old. And they were shocked with great astonishment. And Jesus charged them straightly that no man should know it, and commanded that something should be given to her to eat.

42. And then he left from there, and came into his own country, and his disciples followed him. In addition, when the Sabbath day came, he began to teach in the synagogue: and all who heard were astonished, saying, 'Where has this *man* come up with these things? What wisdom *is* this, which is given to him that produces these mighty works that are done by his hands? Is this not the carpenter, the son of Mary, the brother of James, and Joses, and of Juda, and Simon? And are not his sisters here with us?' And they were offended by him.

43. However, Jesus said to them, "**A prophet is honored by all, except in his own country, and among his own kin, and in his own house.**" In addition, he could do no mighty work there, except that he laid his hands upon a few sick folk, and healed *them*. And he marveled because of their unbelief. And he went round about the villages, teaching.

44. And he called *to him* the twelve, and began to send them forth by two and two. He gave them power over unclean spirits; And commanded them that they should take nothing for *their* journey, save a staff only; no script, no bread, no money in *their* purse: And that they *be* shod with sandals; and not put on two coats. And he said to them, "**In whatever place you enter into a house, stay there till you depart from that place. And whoever will not receive you, nor hear you, when you depart, shake off the dust under your feet for a testimony against them. Verily I say unto you, It will be more tolerable for Sodom and Gomorrha in the Day of Judgment, than for that city.**" And they went out, and preached that men should repent.
45. They cast out many devils, and anointed many with oil who were sick, and healed *them*. King Herod heard *of him;* (for Jesus' name had spread abroad: and Herod said, that it was John the Baptist who had risen from the dead, and therefore mighty works show forth themselves in him. Others said that it is Elias. And others said, that it was a prophet, or the return of one of the prophets. But when Herod heard of it, he said, 'It is John, who I beheaded: he is risen from the dead.'
46. For Herod himself had sent forth and laid hold upon John, and bound him in prison for Herodias' sake, his brother Philip's wife: for he had married her. Because John had told Herod, 'It is not lawful for you to have your brother's wife and called her a whore'. Therefore, Herodias had a quarrel against him, and wanted to have him killed; but she could not, because Herod feared John, knowing that he was a just man and a holy man. Herod had observed him;

and listened to him, and saw that he did many good things, and heard him gladly.

47. However, Herod was taken with Herodias' daughter, Salome, and he swore to her, 'Whatever you will ask of me, I will give you, up to half of my kingdom'. And her mother said, 'The head of John the Baptist.' And she came in straightway with haste to the king, and said, 'I ask that you give me the head of John the Baptist on a platter'.

48. And the king was exceedingly sorry; *yes,* for his oath's sake, and for the sake of those who sat with him, but he could not reject her. And immediately the king sent an executioner, and commanded that John's head should be brought, and the executioner went and beheaded him in the prison, and brought his head on a platter, and gave it to the damsel: and the damsel gave it to her mother. When John's disciples heard about it, they came and took up his corpse, and laid it in a tomb.

49. Johns' apostles gathered themselves together about Jesus, and told him all things, both what they had done, and what they had taught. And he said to them, **"Take yourselves apart into a desert place, and rest a while."** for there were many coming and going, and they had no leisure so much as to eat.

50. And Jesus and his disciples departed into a desert place by ship privately. When the people saw them departing, as many knew of him, they ran afoot out of the cities, and they came together before him. And Jesus, when he came out, saw the many people, and was moved with compassion toward them, because they were as sheep without a shepherd: and he began to teach them many

things. And when the day was far spent, his disciples came to him, and said, 'This is a desert place, and now it is late: Send them away, so that they may go into the country round about, and into the villages, and buy themselves bread: for they have nothing to eat.'

51. He answered and said to them, "**You give them something to eat!**" And they said to him, 'Should we go and buy two hundred pennyworth of bread, and give it to them to eat?' He said to them, "**How many loaves do you have? Go and see.**" And when they returned, they said, five, and two fish. He commanded them to make all the people sit down by companies upon the green grass, and they sat down in ranks, by hundreds, and by fifties. Then he took the five loaves and the two fishes, he looked up to heaven, and blessed them and broke the loaves, and gave *them* to his disciples to set before them; and the two fishes he divided among them all. Thus did they all eat, and were filled.

52. They took up twelve baskets full of the fragments, and of the fishes. And they that ate of the loaves were about five thousand people. And straightway he constrained his disciples to get into the ship, and to go to the other side before to Bethsaida, while he sent the people away.

53. When he had sent them away, he departed into a mountain to pray. In addition, when evening came, the ship was in the midst of the sea, and he was alone on the land. In addition, he saw them toiling and rowing; for the wind was contrary to them. Then, about the fourth watch of the night, he came to them, walking upon the sea, and would have passed by them. But when they saw him

walking upon the sea, they supposed it was a spirit, and they cried out.

54. For they all saw him, and were troubled. But, immediately he talked to them, and said, "**Be of good cheer: it is I; be not afraid."** And he went to them and got into the ship; and the wind ceased, and they were extremely amazed beyond measure, and wondered. For they had not considered *the miracle* of the loaves, because their hearts were hardened. And when they had passed the sea, they came to the land of Gennesaret, and drew to the shore.

55. And when they came out of the ship, straightway the people there knew of him and ran through that whole region round about, and began to carry about the beds of those who were sick to where they heard he was. And wherever he went, into villages, or cities, or country, they laid the sick in the streets, and pleaded with him that they might touch, even the border of his garment; and as many as touched him were made whole.

56. Then the Pharisees came together about him, and with certain of the scribes who came from Jerusalem. When they saw some of his disciples eat bread with defiled, that is to say, with unwashed, hands, they found fault. For the Pharisees and all the Jews, unless they wash *their* hands often, they were prohibited from eating, holding the tradition of the elders. And *when they come* from the market, they did not wash. And many other such things, which they have received from scripture to hold, such *as* the washing of cups, and pots, brass vessels, and of tables. Then the Pharisees and scribes asked him, 'Why do your

disciples disregard the tradition of the elders, and eat bread with unwashed hands?'

57. Jesus answered, **"Correctly, has Esaias prophesied of you hypocrites, as it is written, these people honored me with *their* lips, but their hearts are far from me. How is it in vain they worship me, teaching *as* doctrines the commandments of men? For laying aside the commandment of God, you hold the tradition of men, *as* the washing of pots and cup as higher, along with many other such things as you do.**

58. **And he said to them, you reject the commandment of God, that you may keep your own traditions. For Moses said, Honor your father and your mother; and, Whoever curses father or mother, let him die: But you say, If a man will say to his father or mother, *It is* free, that is to say, a gift, by whatever you might profited from me; *he will be free.* In addition, you suffer him to do nothing more for his father or his mother. Making the word of God of no effect through your tradition, which you have established: and the many other things that you do like that."**

59. And when he had called all the people to him, he said to them, **"Listen to me every one *of you,* and understand!" There is nothing from outside a man, which entering into him can defile him: but the things that come out of him, those are the things that defile the man. If any man has ears to hear, let him hear!"**

60. And when he entered into the house of the people, his disciples asked him concerning the parable. He said to them, **"Are you also without understanding also? Do you**

not perceive, that whatever thing from outside that enters into a man cannot defile him; because it entered not into his heart, but into the belly, and goes out into the sewer, purging all meats?" And he said, "That which comes out of the man that is what defiles the man. For from within, out of the heart of men, proceed evil thoughts, adulteries, fornications, murders, Thefts, covetousness, wickedness, deceit, lasciviousness, an evil eye, blasphemy, pride, foolishness: All these evil things come from within, and defiles the man."

61. And from there he arose, and went into the borders of Tyre and Sidon, and entered into a house, and would have no man know *it:* but he could not hide. For a *certain* woman, whose young daughter had an unclean spirit, heard of him, and came and fell at his feet: The woman was a Greek, a Syrophenician by nation; and she begged him that he might cast forth the devil out of her daughter. However, Jesus said to her, **"Let the children first be filled: for it is not right to take the children's bread, and to cast *it* to the dogs."** And she answered and said to him, 'Yes, Lord: let the dogs under the table eat of the children's crumbs.' And he said to her, **"For saying this, go your way; the devil is gone out of your daughter".** And when she came to her house, she found the devil gone out, and her daughter laid upon the bed.

62. Again, departing from the coasts of Tyre and Sidon, he came to the Sea of Galilee, through the midst of the coasts of Decapolis. And they brought him one who was deaf, and had an impediment in his speech; and they asked him to put his hand upon him. And he took him aside from the

multitude, and put his fingers into his ears, and he spit, and touched his tongue; and looking up to heaven, he sighed, and said unto him, "**Ephphatha**", that is, "**be opened."** Straightway his ears were opened, and the string of his tongue was loosed, and he spoke plainly. And he cautioned them that they should tell no man: but the more he charged them, so much the more they spread *It*. The people were astonished beyond measure, saying, He has done all things well: he made both the deaf to hear, and the dumb to speak.

63. On that day, the multitude was very great, and having nothing to eat, Jesus called his disciples *to him,* and said to them**, "I have compassion on the multitude, because they have now been with me three days, and have had nothing to eat. And if I send them away fasting to their own houses, they will faint by the way: for many of them came from far."** And his disciples questioned him, 'By what means can a man satisfy these *men* with bread here in the wilderness?' Jesus then asked them, "**How many loaves do you have?"**

64. They said, 'Seven.' And he commanded the people to sit down on the ground: and he took the seven loaves, gave thanks, broke them, and gave them to his disciples to set before *them;* and they set *them* before the people. They had a few small fishes, and he blessed them, and commanded that they also be set before *them*. Therefore, they ate, and were filled: and they took up seven baskets of broken *meat* that was left. They that had eaten were about four thousand, and he sent them away.

65. Straightway he entered onto a ship with his disciples, and came into the port at Dalmanutha. And the Pharisees came forth, and began to question with him, seeking from him a sign from heaven, tempting him. And he sighed deeply in his spirit, and said, **"Why does this generation seek after a sign? Verily, I say unto you, there will no sign be given unto this generation."** And he left them, and entering into the ship again departed to the other side.

66. Now the disciples had forgotten to take bread, they had in the ship only one loaf. Then he told them, saying, **"Take heed; beware of the leaven of the Pharisees, and of the leaven of Herod"**. And the disciples reasoned among themselves, saying, 'Is it because we have no bread that he said this?' And when Jesus heard it, he said to them, **"Why do reason so, because you have no bread? Do you neither perceive, nor understand? Have you so hardened your heart? Having eyes, can you not see? And having ears, can you not hear? In addition, do you not remember when I broke the five loaves among five thousand, how many baskets full of fragments you took up?** They said to him, 'Twelve.', **And as of the seven fish among four thousand, how many baskets full of fragments took you up?"** And they said, 'Seven.' And he said to them, **"How is it that you did not understand me when I spoke of 'bread'?"**

67. As he came to Bethsaida, they brought a blind man to him, and asked him to touch him. And he took the blind man by the hand, and led him out of the town; and when he had spit on his eyes, and put his hands upon him, he asked him if he saw anything. And he looked up, and said, 'I see men as trees, walking'. After that, he put *his* hands again upon

his eyes, and made him look up: and he was restored, and saw every man clearly. And he sent him away to his house, saying, "**Do not go into the town, or tell** *it* **to anyone in the town**".

68. And Jesus went out, and his disciples, into the towns of Caesarea Philippi: and by the way, he asked his disciples, saying to them, "**Who do men say that I am?**" And they answered, 'John the Baptist: but some *say,* Elias; and others, one of the prophets'. And he said to them, "**But, who do you say that I am?**" And Peter answered and said to him, 'You are the Christ.' And Jesus charged them that they should tell no man about him.

69. And he began to teach them that the Son of man must suffer many things, and be rejected of the elders, and the chief priests, and the scribes, and be killed, and after three days rise again. He spoke openly saying that, and Peter took him on, and began to rebuke him. However, when he had turned about and looked on his disciples, he rebuked Peter, saying, "**Get you behind me, Satan: for you savor not the things that are of God, but the things that are of men.**"

70. And when he had called the people *to him* along with his disciples, he said to them, "**Whoever will come after me, let him deny himself, and take up his cross, and follow me. For whoever will save his life will lose it; but whosoever will lose his life for my sake and the gospel's, the same will save it. For what will it profit a man, if he will gain the whole world, and lose his own soul? Or what will a man give in exchange for his soul? Therefore whoever will be ashamed of me and of my words in this**

adulterous and sinful generation, of him also will the Son of man be ashamed, when he comes into the glory of his Father with the holy angels."

71. And he said to them, "**Verily, I say to you, that there are some of you that stand here, who will not taste of death, till they have seen the kingdom of God come with power.**"

72. And after six days, Jesus took Peter, James, and John *with him*, and led them up onto a high mountain apart by themselves: and he was transfigured before them. And his clothes became shining, exceeding white as snow; so as no fuller on earth can white them. And there Elias with Moses appeared unto them talking with Jesus.

73. And Peter answered and said to Jesus, 'Master; it is good for us to be here: and let us make three tabernacles; one for you, and one for Moses, and one for Elias'. (He said this because he did not know what else to say for they were very afraid.) Then a cloud descended that overshadowed them: and a voice came out of the cloud, saying, 'This is my beloved Son: hear him.' Then suddenly, when they looked round about, they saw no man, except Jesus and themselves.

74. And as they came down from the mountain, he charged them that they should tell no man what things they had seen, till the Son of man were risen from the dead. And they kept that saying among themselves, questioning one with another about what the rising from the dead meant. And they asked him, saying, 'Why do the scribes say that Elias must first come'? And he answered and told them, **"Elias verily came first, and restored all things; and how it**

is written of the Son of man, that he must suffer many things, and be set at naught. But I say unto you, that Elias is indeed come, but they did not see him, and they have done unto him whatever was listed, as it is written in the scriptures."

75. And when he came back to *his* other disciples, he saw a great multitude about them, and the scribes questioning with them. And straightway all the people, when they beheld him, were greatly amazed, and ran to *him* and saluted him. And Jesus asked the scribes, "**What are you questioning them about?**"

76. And one of the multitude answered and said, 'Master, I have brought to you my son, who has a dumb spirit; and whenever he takes him, he tears him: and he foams, gnashes his teeth, and pines away I spoke to your disciples that they should cast him out; and they could not'.

77. Jesus answered, and said**, "O faithless generation, how long will I be with you? How long will I suffer you? Bring him to me."** And they brought him to him: and when he saw him, straightway the spirit tore at him and put him on the ground, and he wallowed around foaming at the mouth. And Jesus asked his father, "**How long ago has it been since this came to him?**" And often it has cast him into the fire, and into the water, to destroy him: but if you can do anything, have compassion on us, and help us.'

78. Jesus said to him**, "It will be done if you can believe that all things *are* possible to he who believes".** Straightway the father of the child cried out, and said with tears, 'Lord, I believe; help me with my unbelief.' When Jesus saw that the people coming, running together, he rebuked the foul

spirit, saying to it, "***You dumb and deaf spirit, I command you, come out of him, and enter no more into him***". And *the spirit* cried, and shook him sore, and came out of him: and he was as one dead, insomuch that many said, 'He is dead.'

79. But Jesus took him by the hand, and lifted him up; and he arose. And when he came into the house, his disciples asked him privately, 'Why could we not cast him out'? And he said to them, **"This kind can come forth by nothing except much prayer and fasting."**

80. And they departed thence, and passed through Galilee; and he desired that no man should know *it*. For he taught his disciples, and said to them, **"The Son of man will be delivered into the hands of men, and they will kill him; and after that he is killed, he will rise the third day."** However, they did not understand that saying, and were afraid to ask him the meaning.

81. And he came to Capernaum, and being in the house he asked them, **"What was it that you disputed among yourselves by the way"**, But they held their peace: because on the way they had disputed among themselves, who *should be* the greatest. In addition, he sat down, called the twelve, and said to them, **"If any man desires to be first, *the same* will be last of all and the servant of all"**.

82. And he took a child, and set him in the midst of them: and when he had taken him in his arms, he said to them, **"Whoever will receive one of such children in my name, receives me: and whoever will receive me, receives not me, but him that sent me."**

83. John asked him, 'Master, we saw one casting out devils in your name, and he did not follow us: and we forbad him, because he did follow us'. But Jesus said, **"Do not forbid him: for there is no man who will do a miracle in my name, who can lightly speak evil of me. For he that is not against us is on our side. For whoever will give you a cup of water to drink in my name, because you belong to Christ, verily I say unto you, he will not lose his reward.**

84. **And whoever will offend one of** *these* **little ones who believe in me, it is better for him that a millstone were hanged about his neck, and he were cast into the sea. And if your hand offends you, cut it off: it is better for you to enter into life maimed, than having two hands to go into hell, into the fire that never will be quenched; where their pain does not die, and the fire is not quenched.**

85. **And if your foot offends you, cut it off: it is better for you to enter halt into life, than having two feet to be cast into hell, into the fire that never will be quenched; where their pain does not die, and the fire is not quenched.**

86. **And if your eye offends you, pluck it out: it is better for you to enter into the kingdom of God with one eye, than having two eyes and be cast into hell fire; where their pain does not die, and the fire is not quenched. For every one will be salted with fire, and every sacrifice will be salted with salt. Salt** *is* **good: but if the salt has lost his saltiness, what will you season with? Have the salt in yourselves, and have peace one with another."**

87. And he arose from there, and came to the coasts of Judaea by the farther side of the Jordan: and the people resorted

to him again; and, as he was used to doing, he taught them again.

88. And the Pharisees came to him, and tempted him, 'Is it lawful for a man to put away *his* wife?' And he answered and said to them, **"What did Moses command you?** They said, 'Moses allowed there to be written a bill of divorcement, and for her to be put away'. Jesus answered and said to them, **"Because of the hardness of your heart, he wrote this precept for you. However, from the beginning of the creation God made them male and female.**

89. **For this cause, will a man leave his father and mother, and cleave to his wife; and the two will be one flesh: so then, they are no more two, but one flesh. What therefore God has joined together, let not man put asunder."**

90. And in the house, his disciples asked him again about the same *matter*. And he said to them, **"Whoever will put away his wife, and marries another, commits adultery against her. And if a woman will put away her husband, and be married to another, she commits adultery."**

91. And they brought young children to him, so that he could touch them: and *his* disciples rebuked those that brought *them*. However, when Jesus saw *it,* he was quite displeased, and said to them, **"Suffer the little children to come to me, and forbid them not: for of such is the kingdom of God. Verily I say to you, whoever will not receive the kingdom of God as a little child, he will not enter therein."** And he took them up in his arms, put *his* hands upon them, and blessed them."

92. And when he was gone forth into the way, there came a man running, who kneeled to him, and asked him, 'Good Master, what will I do that I may inherit eternal life'? Jesus said to him, **"Why do you call me good?** *There is* **none good but one,** *that is,* **God. You know the commandments, do not commit adultery, do not kill, and do not steal, do not bear false witness. Do not defraud, and honor your father and mother."** And the man answered and said to him, 'Master, all these have I observed from my youth'.

93. Then Jesus beholding him loved him, and said to him, **"One thing you lack: go your way, sell whatever you have, and give to the poor, so you will have treasure in heaven, and come, take up the cross, and follow me."** And the man was saddened at that saying, and went away grieved, for he had great possessions.

94. "And Jesus looked round about, and said to his disciples, **"How difficult it will be for they who have riches to enter into the kingdom of God!** And the disciples were astonished at his words. But Jesus answered again, and said to them, **"Children, how hard is it for them that trust in riches to enter into the kingdom of God! It is easier for a camel to go through the eye of a needle, than for a rich man to enter into the kingdom of God."**

95. And they were astonished out of measure, saying among themselves, 'Who then can be saved?' And Jesus looked upon them and said, **"With men** *it is* **impossible, but not with God: for with God all things are possible."**

96. Then Peter began to say to him, 'Lo, we have left all, and have followed you.' And Jesus answered and said, **"Verily, I**

say to you, There is no man who has left house, or brothers, or sisters, or father, or mother, or wife, or children, or lands, for my sake, and the gospel's, except he will receive an hundredfold now in this time of, houses, and brothers, sisters, mothers, children and lands and persecutions, and in the world to come eternal life. And many *that are* first will be last; and the last shall be first'."

97. Then they were on the way, going up to Jerusalem. Jesus went before them: and they were amazed; and as they followed, they were afraid. He took the twelve aside again and began to tell them what things would happen to him. Saying, **"Behold, we go up to Jerusalem; and the Son of man will be delivered unto the chief priests, and unto the scribes, and they will condemn him to death and will deliver him to the Gentiles. And they will mock him, and will scourge him, and will spit upon him, and will kill him, and on the third day he will rise again."**

98. James and John, the sons of Zebedee, came to him, saying, 'Master, we ask that you should do for us what we wish.' And he said to them, **"What do you want me to do for you?"** They said to him, 'Grant to us that we may sit, one on your right hand, and the other on your left hand, in your glory'. But Jesus said to them, **"You know not what you ask: can you drink from the cup that I drink from? And be baptized with the baptism that I am baptized with? You will indeed drink of the cup that I drink of; and with the baptism that I am baptized you will also be baptized: But to sit on my right hand and on my left hand**

is not mine to give; but *it will be given to them* for whom it is prepared."

99. Moreover, when the disciples heard *it,* they began to be much displeased with James and John. But Jesus called them *to him,* and said to them, **"You know that they who are accounted to rule over the Gentiles exercise lordship over them; and their great ones exercise authority upon them. However, it will not so be among you: but whoever will be great among you, will be your minister: And whosoever of you will be the chief, will be servant of all. For even the Son of man came not to be ministered to, but to minister and to give his life as ransom for many."**

100. And they came to Jericho: and as he went into Jericho with his disciples and a great number of people including blind Bareimaeus, the son of Timaeus, who sat by the highway side begging. And when he heard that it was Jesus of Nazareth, he began to cry out, and say, 'Jesus, *you* Son of David, have mercy on me'. And many criticized him, saying that he should hold his peace: but he cried out a great deal louder, '*You* Son of David have mercy on me'.

101. And Jesus stood still, and commanded him to be brought. And they called the blind man, saying to him, be of good comfort, rise; he calls you. And he, casting away his garment, rose, and came to Jesus. And Jesus answered and said to him**, "What do you want for me to do for you?"** The blind man said to him, 'Lord, I wish that I might receive my sight'. Then Jesus said to him, "**Go your way; your faith hath made you whole**". And immediately he received his sight, and he followed Jesus in the way.

102. And when they came near to Jerusalem, by Bethphage and Bethany, at the Mount of Olives, he sent forth two of his disciples, and said to them, "**Go into the village over there: and as soon as you have entered into it, you will find a colt tied, upon which no man ever sat; loose him, and bring** *him*. **Moreover, if any man says to you, 'Why do you do this'? Say you that the Lord has need of him; and straightway he will send him here.**"

103. And on the next day, when they came from Bethany, he was hungry: And seeing a fig tree afar off having leaves, he came, hoping that he might find something on it. When he came to it, he found nothing but leaves, for the time of figs had not come, and Jesus said to it, "**No man will eat fruit of you hereafter forever.**" And his disciples heard *it*.

104. When they got to Jerusalem, Jesus went into the temple, and began to cast out those who sold and bought in the temple, and overthrew the tables of the moneychangers, and the seats of those who sold doves. And he would not allow anyone to carry *any* vessel through the temple.

105. And he taught, saying to them, "**Is it not written, my house will be called of all nations the house of prayer? But you have made it a den of thieves**." And the scribes and chief priests heard *it,* and thought about how they might destroy him: for they feared him, because all the people were astonished at his doctrine. When evening came, he went out of the city.

106. In the morning, as they passed by, they saw that the fig tree had dried up from the roots. And Peter calling to remembrance said to him, Master, 'behold, the fig tree that you cursed is withered away.'

107. And Jesus said to them, **"Have faith in God. For verily I say to you, That whoever will say to this mountain, Be removed, and be cast into the sea; and will not doubt in his heart, but will believe that those things which he said will come to pass; he will have whatever he said. Therefore, I say to you, whatever things you desire, when you pray, believe that you will receive** *them,* **and you will have** *them.* **In addition, when you stand praying, forgive, if you have anything against anyone, so that your Father who is also in heaven may forgive you and your trespasses. But if you do not forgive, neither will your Father which is in the heaven within your hearts forgive you your trespasses."**

108. They returned to Jerusalem: and as he was walking in the temple, the chief priests came to him along with the scribes, and the elders, and said to him, 'By what authority do you do these things? And who gave you this authority to do these things'? And Jesus answered and said to them, **'I will also ask of you one question, and answer me, and I will tell you by what authority I do these things. The baptism of John, was** *it* **from heaven, or of men? Answer me."**

109. In addition, the priests reasoned with themselves, saying, 'If we will say, from heaven; he will say, why then did you not believe him?' However, they could not say, 'of men' because they feared the people: for all *men* counted John as a prophet indeed. They responded and said to Jesus, 'We cannot tell.' And Jesus replied, saying to them, **"Neither will I tell you by what authority I do these things."**

110. And he began to speak to them in parables. "**A *certain* man planted a vineyard, and set a hedge about *it*, and dug *a place for* the wine vat, and built a tower, and let it out to husbandmen, and went into a far country.** And at the season, he sent to the husbandmen a servant that he might receive from the husbandmen of the fruit of the vineyard. And they caught the servant and beat him, and sent *him* away empty.
111. Again, he sent another servant to them; and they cast stones at him, wounded *him* in the head, and sent *him* away shamefully handled. Again he sent another; and him they killed, and many others; beating some, and killing some.
112. Having only one son, his well beloved, he sent him also lastly to them, saying, they will respect my son. But those husbandmen said among themselves, this is the heir; come, let us kill him, and the inheritance will be ours. And they took him, killed him, and cast his body out of the vineyard.
113. **Therefore, what do you think the lord of the vineyard do? He will come and destroy the husbandmen, and will give the vineyard unto others. Have you not read this scripture? The stone which the builders rejected is become the head of the corner: This was the Lord's doing, and it is marvelous in our eyes?"** And the Pharisees sought to lay hold on him, but feared the people: for they knew that he had spoken the parable against them: but they left him, and went their way.
114. And they sent to him certain of the Pharisees and of the Herodians, to catch him in *his* words. And when they came,

they said to him, 'Master, we know that you are true, and fear no man: for you do not regard the person of men, but teach the way of God in truth. Is it lawful to give tribute to Caesar, or not? Will we give, or will we not give'?

115. But he, knowing their hypocrisy, said to them, **"Why do you tempt me? Bring me a penny, so that I may see** *it.***"** And they brought *it*. And he said to them, **"Whose this image and superscription is this?"** And they answered, Caesar's. And Jesus in answer said, **"Render unto Caesar the things that are Caesar's, and unto God the things that are God's."** And they marveled at him.

116. Then the Sadducees came to him, (who say there is no resurrection); and they asked him, 'Rabbi, Moses wrote to us, If a man's brother die, and leaves *his* wife *behind him,* and leaves no children, and his brother should take his wife, and father children for his brother (as is required by the Law).

117. Now there were seven brothers: and the first took a wife, and dying left no seed. And the second took her, and died, neither did he leave any children: and the third likewise. And the seven had her, and left no seed: lastly, the woman died also. In the resurrection therefore, when they will rise, whose wife will she be of them? For the seven had her to wife.

118. Jesus answered, saying to them, **"You are in error, because you do not know the scriptures, or the power of God! For when they will rise from the dead, they neither marry, nor are given in marriage; but are as the angels, which are in heaven. And as regarding the dead, that is, they that they rise. Have you not read in the book of Moses, how in**

the bush God spoke unto him, saying, I *am* the God of Abraham, and the God of Isaac, and the God of Jacob? He is not the God of the dead, but the God of the living: Therefore you greatly err."

119. And one of the scribes came, and having heard them reasoning together, and perceiving that he had answered them well, asked him, 'Which is the first commandment of all'? And Jesus answered him, **"The first of all the commandments *is,* Hear, O Israel; the Lord our God is One: And you will love the Lord your God with all your heart, and with all your soul, and with all your mind, and with all your strength: this is the first commandment. And the second *is namely* this; you will love your neighbor as yourself. There are no other commandments greater than these."** And the scribe said to him, 'Well said Master, you have spoken the truth. For there is one God; and there is none other than He and we should love Him with all the heart, and with all the understanding, and with all the soul, and with all the strength And to love *his* neighbor as himself, is more than all whole burnt offerings and sacrifices'. And when Jesus saw that he answered discreetly, he said to him, **"You are not far from the kingdom of God."** And no man after that dared to ask him *any question.*

120. And Jesus taught further, while in the temple and said, **"How can the scribes say that Christ is the Son of David? For David himself said by the Holy Ghost, "The Lord said to my Lord, Sit you on my right hand, till I make your enemies your footstool." David therefore himself called**

him Lord; how then is he his son? And the common people heard him gladly."

121. And he told them this doctrine, **"Beware of the scribes, who love to go in long clothing, and** *love* **salutations in the marketplaces, and the chief seats in the synagogues, and the uppermost rooms at feasts: Who devour widows' houses, and for a pretence make long prayers: these will receive greater damnation."**

122. And Jesus sat over by the treasury, and beheld how the people cast money into the treasury: and how many that were rich cast in much. Then there came a certain poor widow, and she threw in two mites, which make a penny. And he called his disciples *to him*, and said to them, **"Verily, I say to you, That this poor widow has cast more in, than all the rich who have cast into the treasury. For all** *they* **did cast in was but a part of their abundance; but she of her own will cast in all that she had,** *even* **all her living."**

123. And as he went out of the temple, one of his disciples said to him, 'Master, see what manner of stones and what buildings *are here!*' And Jesus answering, said to him, **"Do you see these great buildings? There will not be left one stone upon another that will not be thrown down."**

124. And as he sat upon the Mount of Olives over against the temple, Peter, James, John, and Andrew asked him privately, 'Tell us, when will these things happen? And what *will be* the sign when all these things will be fulfilled?'

125. And Jesus answered them, **"Take heed lest any** *man* **deceive you: For many will come in my name, saying, I am** *Christ;* **and will deceive many. And when you will hear**

of wars and rumors of wars, do not be troubled: for *such things* are necessary; but the end *will* is not in doubt. For nation will rise against nation, and kingdom against kingdom: and there will be earthquakes in diverse places, and there will be famines and troubles: these *are* the beginnings of sorrows.

126. However, take heed for yourselves: for they will deliver you up to councils; and in the synagogues you will be beaten: and you will be brought before rulers and kings for my sake, for a testimony against them. And the gospel must first be published among all nations. But when they will lead *you* and deliver you up, take no thought beforehand what you will speak, neither should you premeditate: but whatever will be given you in that hour, speak that.

127. For it is not you who speaks, but the Holy Ghost. Now brother will betray the brother to death, and the father the son; and children will rise up against *their* parents, and will cause them to be put to death and you will be hated of all *men* for my name's sake: but he that will endure unto the end, the will be saved.

128. However, when you will see the abomination of desolation, spoken of by Daniel the prophet, standing where it ought not, (let him that read, and understand,) then let them that be in Judaea flee to the mountains. And let him that is on the housetop not go down into the house, neither return within to take anything out of his house. And let him that is in the field not turn back again for to take up his garment.

129. But woe to them that are with child, and to them that give suck in those days! And pray you that your flight not happen in the winter. For *in* those days will be affliction, such as was not from the beginning of the creation of God until this time, or the future. And except that the Lord had shortened those days, no flesh should be saved: but for the elect's sake, who he has chosen, he has shortened the days.

130. And then if any man will say to you, Lo, here *is* Christ; or, lo, *he is* there; believe *him* not: For false Christs and false prophets will rise, and will show signs and wonders, to seduce, if *it were* possible, even the elect. But take heed! Behold, I have foretold you all things.

131. But in those days, after that tribulation, the sun will be darkened, and the moon will not give her light, and the stars of heaven will fall, and the powers that are in heaven will be shaken. Then they will see the Son of man coming in the clouds with great power and glory. Then he will send his angels, and will gather together his elect from the four winds, from the uttermost part of the earth to the uttermost parts of heaven.

132. Now learn a parable of the fig tree; When her branch is thus tender, and puts forth leaves, you know that summer is near: So in like manner when you will see these things come to pass, know that it is near, *even* at the door! Verily, I say to you, that this generation will not pass, until all these things are done. Heaven and earth will pass away: but my words will not pass away.

133. But of that day and *that* hour that no man knows, no, not even the angels who are in heaven, or even the Son, but

the Father. Take heed, watch and pray: for you know not when the time is! *For the Son of man is* as a man taking a far journey, who left his house, and gave authority to his servants, and to every man his work, and commanded the porter to watch.

134. Therefore, watch! For you do not know when the master of the house will come, at evening, or at midnight, or at the cockcrowing, or in the morning. Lest he coming suddenly he find you sleeping. What I say to you I say to all, is be watchful!"

135. After two days was *the feast of* the Passover, and of the unleavened bread: and the chief priests and the scribes sought how they might take him by trickery, and put *him* to death. But they said, 'Not on the feast *day,* because there might be an uproar from the people'.

136. And being in Bethany in the house of Simon the leper, as he sat at meat, there came a woman having an alabaster box of ointment of spices that were very precious; and she opened the box, and poured *it* on his head.

137. And there were some disciples who were indignant within themselves, and said, 'Why was this waste of ointment made'? For it might have been sold for more than three hundred pence, and have been given to the poor.' And they murmured against her.

138. However, Jesus said, "**Let her alone; why trouble her? She has done good work on me. For you will have the poor with you always, and whenever you choose you may do them good: but you will not always have me. She has done the best she could. She is come beforehand to anoint my body for the burial. Verily, I say to you,**

wherever this gospel will be preached throughout the whole world, *what* she has done will be spoken of as a memorial of her."

139. And Judas Iscariot, one of the twelve, went to the chief priests, to betray him to them. And when they heard this, they were glad, and promised to give him money. And he sought how he might conveniently betray him.

140. On the first day of unleavened bread, during the celebration of Passover, his disciples said to him, 'Where do you want us to go to prepare for the Passover meal'? And he sent forth two of his disciples, and said to them, **"Go you into the city, and there you will meet a man bearing a pitcher of water: follow him. Wherever he goes in, say to the good man of the house, The Master said, 'here is the guest chamber where I will eat the Passover with my disciples.' and he will show you a large upper room furnished** *and* **prepared, make ready for us there."**

141. And his disciples went forth, and came into the city, and found it as he had said to them, and they made ready for the Passover. And in the evening he arrived with the twelve. And as they sat and ate, Jesus said, **"Verily I say unto you, one of you which eats with me will betray me"**. And they began to be sorrowful, and said to him one by one, *Is* it I? And another said, 'Is it I'? And he answered and said to them, **"***It is* **one of you twelve, who dips with me in the dish. Indeed, it will happen to the Son of man as it is written of him: but woe to that man by whom the Son of man is betrayed! It would be better for that man if he had never been born."**

142. And as they ate, Jesus took the bread, and blessed, and broke *it,* and gave to them, and said, "**Take, eat: this is my body.**" And he took the cup, and when he had given thanks, he gave *it* to them: and they all drank of it. And he said to them, "**This is my blood of the New Testament, which is shed for many. Verily< I say to you, I will drink no more of the fruit of the vine, until that day that I drink it again in the kingdom of God.**"

143. And when they had sung a hymn, they went out onto the Mount of Olives. And Jesus said to them, "**All of you will be accosted because of me this night: for it is written, 'I will smite the shepherd, and the sheep will be scattered. But after that I am risen, I will go before you into Galilee.'**"

144. But Peter said to him, 'Although all the others might be offended, but I *will* not'. And Jesus said to him, "**Verily, I say unto you, that this day,** *even* **in this night, before the cock crows twice, you will deny me thrice.**" However, peter spoke the more strongly, 'If I should die with you, I will not deny you in any way'! Likewise, the other disciples said the same thing.

145. Then they went to a place that was named Gethsemane, and he said to his disciples**, "Sit here while I pray".** And he took with him Peter, James, and John, and began to be very amazed and very depressed; and said to them, "**My soul is exceeding sorrowful unto death: wait here, and watch.**" And he went forward a little, and fell on the ground, and prayed that, if it were possible, the hour might pass from him. Then, after a moment, he said, "**Alas, Father, all things** *are* **possible unto you; take away this**

cup from me: nevertheless it is not what I will, but what you will."

146. When he returned, and found them sleeping, and said to Simon Peter, **"Are you asleep? Could you not watch one hour? Watch you and pray, lest you enter into temptation. The spirit truly *is* ready, but the flesh *is* weak."**

147. Again, he went away, and prayed, and spoke the same words. When he returned, he found them asleep again, (for their eyes were heavy,) neither of them knew what to answer him. Then he came the third time, and said to them, **"Sleep on now, and take *your* rest: it is enough, the hour is come; behold, the Son of man has been betrayed into the hands of sinners. Rise up, let us go; lo, he that betrayed me is at hand."**

148. And immediately, while he thus spoke, Judas came, one of the twelve, and with him a great multitude with swords and staves, with the chief priest and the scribes and the elders. And the one that betrayed him had given them a signal, saying, 'Whoever I kiss, that is he; take him, and lead *him* away safely'. And as soon as he came, he went straightway to him, and said, 'Master, master'; and kissed him.

149. And they laid their hands on him, and took him. And one of them that stood by drew a sword, and swung on a servant of the high priest, and cut off his ear. And Jesus spoke out and said to them, **"Have you come out as against a thief, with swords and *with* staves to take me? I was with you daily in the temple teaching, and you didn't take me."** He added, **"The scriptures must be fulfilled."**

150. Then all of his disciples forsook him, and fled. Then a certain young man followed him, having a linen cloth cast about *his* naked *body;* and the young men in the crowd laid hold on him: And he left the linen cloth, and fled from them naked.
151. They led Jesus away to the high priest: and with him were assembled all the chief priests, the elders and the scribes. Peter followed from afar off, even into the palace of the high priest, and he sat with the servants, and warmed himself at the fire. The chief priests and all the council sought for witness against Jesus to put him to death; and found none. Many bore false witness against him, but their testimonies were in disagreement.
152. Then there arose certain men who bore false witness against him, saying, 'We heard him say, I will destroy this temple that is made with hands, and within three days I will build another made without hands'. But neither did those witnesses agree together. And the high priest stood up in the midst, and asked Jesus, 'Why do you not answer us? *Is it or is it not true what* these witnesses say against you?'
153. Nevertheless, Jesus held his peace, and answered nothing. Again, the high priest asked him, and said to him, Are you the Christ, the Son of the Blessed? And Jesus said, "**I am: and you will see the Son of man sitting on the right hand of power, and coming in the clouds of heaven.**"
154. Then the high priest tore at his clothes, and said, 'Why do we need any further witnesses? You have heard the blasphemy: what do you all think?' And they all condemned him to be guilty to death. Moreover, some

began to spit on him, to cover up his face, to buffet him, and to say to him, 'Heresy' and the servants slapped him with the palms of their hands.

155. And as Peter was beneath in the palace, there came one of the house cleaners of the high priest: And when she saw Peter warming himself, she looked upon him, and said, 'You were also with Jesus of Nazareth.' But he denied it, saying, 'I don't know, nor do I understand what you say'. And another maid saw him later, and she began to say to them that stood by, 'This is *one* of them.' And he denied it again.

156. A little later, those who stood by said again to Peter, 'Surely, you are *one* of them: for you are a Galilean, your accent agrees *with that*'. But he began to curse and to swear, *saying,* 'I don't know this man about whom you speak'. And the cock crowed the second time, and Peter called to mind the word that Jesus said to him earlier, **"Before the cock crows twice, you will deny me three times."** And when Peter thought about it, he wept.

157. Straightway in the morning, the chief priests held a consultation with the elders and scribes and the whole council, and had Jesus tied up, and carried *him* away, and delivered *him* to Pilate. Pilate asked him, 'Are you the King of the Jews'? Pilate asked him again, saying, 'Why don't you answer? Behold how many things they witness against you.' However, Jesus still answered nothing; and Pilate marveled.

158. Now during *the Passover* celebration it was the custom to release to the people one prisoner, whomever they desired. And there was *one* named Barabbas, *who lay*

bound with them that had made insurrection with him, and who had committed murder in the insurrection. And the multitude, crying aloud, began to ask Pilate to *do* what the custom required.

159. However, Pilate answered them, saying, 'Do you wish me to release the King of the Jews to you? (For he knew that the chief priests had delivered Jesus from envy.) But the chief priests moved the people to ask that he should release Barabbas to them. Pilate answered and said again to them, 'What do you wish for me to do to this one who is called the 'King of the Jews'. And they cried out again, 'Crucify him!' Then Pilate said to them, 'Why, what evil has he done?' And they cried out more exceedingly, 'Crucify him!'

160. Therefore, Pilate, willing to content the people, released Barabbas to them, and delivered Jesus, after he had admonished *him,* to be crucified. Then the soldiers called the Praetorian Guard led him away into the hall, and they called together the whole crowds. They clothed him with purple, and braided a crown of thorns, and put it on his *head,* and began to salute him, 'Hail, King of the Jews!' Moreover, they hit him on the head with a reed, spat on him, and feigned bowing *their* knees in worship to him, and after that they mocked him.

161. Then they took the purple robe off him, put his own clothes on him, and led him out to be crucified. And they compelled one Simon, a Cyrenian, who passed by, coming out of the country, the father of Alexander and Rufus, to bear his cross. And they brought him to the place called Golgotha, which is interpreted as the place of the skull.

And they gave him wine mingled with myrrh to drink: but he did not drink. After they put him up on his cross, they paraded his garments, casting lots over them to decide what each man should take, and in the third hour, they nailed him to the cross.

162. The superscription of his accusation was written over his head, 'THE KING OF THE JEWS (INRI)'. In addition, they crucified two thieves with him, one on his right hand, and the other on his left. In addition, the scripture was fulfilled, and they were numbered with the transgressors. And they that passed by railed on him, wagging their heads, and saying, 'Ah, you that destroyed the temple, and built *it* in three days, Save yourself, and come down from the cross'.

163. Likewise the chief priests mockingly said among themselves and the scribes, 'He saved others; why can he not save himself? Let Christ the King of Israel descend now from the cross that we may see and believe.' And the ones who were crucified with him said disrespectful things about him.

164. And when the sixth hour came, there was darkness over the whole land until the ninth hour. And at the ninth hour, Jesus cried with a loud voice, saying, **"Eloi, Eloi, lama sabachthani?"** which is, being interpreted, is, **"My God, my God, why hast you forsaken me?"** And some of them that stood by, when they heard *it,* said, 'Behold, he calls Elias.' And one ran and filled a sponge full of vinegar, and put *it* on a reed, and gave to him to drink, saying, 'Let him alone; let us see whether Elias will come to take him down'. And the veil of the temple was rent in two from the top to the bottom.

165. Finally, He said to them, **"Go into the entire world, and preach the gospel to every creature. He that believeth and is baptized will be saved; but he that believeth not will be damned. Moreover, these signs will follow them that believe; in my name will they cast out devils; they will speak with new tongues. They will take up serpents; and if they drink any deadly thing, it will not hurt them; they will lay hands on the sick, and they will recover."**
166. So then, after the Lord had spoken to them, he was received up into heaven, and sat on the right hand of God. And they went forth, and preached everywhere, the Lord working with *them,* and confirming the word with signs following. Amen.

The Words of Jesus According to the Apostle Luke

1. And, it came to pass, that after three days they found him in the temple, sitting in the midst of the doctors, both hearing them, and asking them questions. And all that heard him were astonished at his understanding and answers. And when they saw him, they were amazed: and his mother said to him, 'Son, why have you done this to us?' Behold, your father and I have sought you with much sorrow.'
2. And he said to them, "**Why is it that you sought me? Don't you know that I must be about my Father's business?**" And they did not understand what he was saying when he spoke to them. But he went down with them, and came to Nazareth, and was subject to them: but his mother kept all these sayings in her heart. And Jesus increased in wisdom and stature, and in favor with God and man.
3. And Jesus being full of the Holy Ghost returned from Jordan, and was led by the Spirit into the wilderness, for forty days being tempted by the devil. And in those days he ate nothing: and when they were ended, he was hungry. And the devil said to him, 'If you are the Son of God, command this stone that it be made bread.. And Jesus answered him, saying, "**It is written, that man will not live by bread alone, but by every word of God**".
4. And the devil, taking him up onto a high mountain, showed to him all the kingdoms of the world in a moment of time. And the devil said to him, 'All this power will I give you and the glory: for that is the power delivered to me; and to

whomever I will I give it. If you will therefore worship me, all of this will be yours.'

5. And Jesus answered and said to him, **"Get you behind me, Satan: for it is written, 'You will only worship the Lord your God, and serve him only.'** Then Satan brought him to Jerusalem, and set him on a pinnacle of the temple, and said to him, 'If you are the Son of God, cast yourself down from here. For it is written, He will give his angels charge over you, to keep you: And in *their* hands they will bear you up, lest at any time you dash your foot against a stone.' And Jesus answering said to him, **"It is said, 'You will not tempt the Lord your God'."** And when the devil had ended all the temptation, he departed from him for a season.

6. And Jesus returned in the power of the Spirit into Galilee: and there went out a fame of him through the entire region round about. And he taught in their synagogues, being glorified by all.

7. And he came to Nazareth, where he had been brought up: and, as his custom was, he went into the synagogue on the Sabbath day, and stood up to read. And there the book of the prophet Esaias was delivered to him. And when he had opened the book, he found the place where it was written, 'The Spirit of the Lord is upon me, because he has anointed me to preach the gospel to the poor. He has sent me to heal the broken hearted, to preach deliverance to the captives, and the recovery of sight to the blind, to set at liberty those who suffer, and to preach the acceptable word of the Lord.'

8. Then he closed the book, and he gave it back to the priest, and sat down. And the eyes of all those who were in the synagogue were fastened on him. And he began to say to them, "**This day, this scripture fulfilled in your ears**". And all bore him witness, and wondered at the gracious words, which proceeded out of his mouth. And they said, 'Is not this Joseph's son'? And he said to them, "**You will surely let me tell this proverb, Physician, heal yourself: whatever we have heard done in Capernaum, I do here in your country also.**"

9. And he said, "**Verily, I say unto you, No prophet is accepted in his own country. But I tell you of the truth, many widows were in Israel in the days of Elias, when the heaven was shut up three years and six months, when great famine was throughout all the land; But unto none of them was Elias sent, save unto Sarepta,** *a city* **of Sidon, to a woman** *who was* **a widow. And many lepers were in Israel in the time of Eliseus the prophet; and none of them was cleansed, except Naaman the Syrian.**"

10. And all in the synagogue, when they heard these things, were filled with wrath, and they rose up, and thrust him out of the city, and led him to the brow of the hill where their city was built, that they might cast him down headlong. However, he passed through the midst of them went his way, and came down to Capernaum, a city of Galilee, and taught there on the Sabbath days. And they were astonished at his doctrine: for his word was with power.

11. And in the synagogue there was a man, who had a spirit of an unclean devil, and cried out with a loud voice, Saying,

'Let *us* alone; what will we to do with you, *you* Jesus of Nazareth? Are you come to destroy us? I know you who you are, the Holy One of God.' And Jesus rebuked him, saying, **"Hold your peace, and come out of him"**. And when the devil had thrown the man to the ground, he came out of him, and hurt him not. And they were all amazed, and spoke among themselves, saying, 'What a teaching this is'! For he commands the unclean spirits with authority and power, and they come out. And his fame spread out into every place of the country round about.'

12. And he arose out of the synagogue, and entered into Simon's house. And Simon's wife's mother was taken with a great fever; and they sought him out for her. And he stood over her, and rebuked the fever; and it left her: and immediately she arose and ministered to them.
13. Now when the sun was setting, all those who were sick with various diseases were brought to him, and he laid his hands on every one of them, and healed them. Moreover, devils also came out of many, crying out saying, 'You are Christ the Son of God'. And he rebuking *them* and did not allow them not to speak: for they knew that he was the Christ.
14. And when it was the next day, he departed and went into a desert place: and the people sought him, and came to him, and stayed with him, so that he should not depart from them. And he said to them, "**I must preach the kingdom of God to other cities also: for therefore I must go.** And he preached in the synagogues of Galilee.
15. And it came to pass, that, as the people pressed upon him to hear the word of God, he stood by the lake of

Gennesaret and he saw two ships standing by the lake, but the fishermen had left them, and were washing *their* nets. He boarded one of the ships, which was Simon's, and prayed to him that he would thrust out a little from the land. In addition, he sat down, and taught the people from the side of the ship.

16. Now when he had finished speaking, he said unto Simon, **Launch out into the deep, and let down your nets for a draught**. And Simon answering said to him, 'Master, we have toiled all the night, and have taken nothing: nevertheless, at your word I will let down the net'. Moreover, when they did this they caught a great multitude of fish and their net broke. And they called to *their* partners, who were in the other ship, that they should come and help them. They came, and filled both the ships, so that they began to sink.

17. When Simon Peter saw *it,* he fell down at Jesus' knees, saying, 'Leave me; for I am a sinful man, O Lord'. For he was astonished, as were all who with him, at the weight of the fish that they had taken. Including James, and John, the sons of Zebedee, who were partners with Simon. And Jesus said to Simon, **"Fear not; from henceforth you will catch men."** And when they had brought their ships to land, they forsook all, and followed him.

18. And it came to pass, when he was in a certain city, he beheld a man full of leprosy: who, on seeing Jesus fell on *his* face, and pleaded with him, saying, 'Lord, if you will, you can make me clean'. And Jesus put forth *his* hand and touched him, saying, **"I will it: be clean."** And immediately the leprosy departed from him. And he charged him to tell

no man: **"but go, and show yourself to the priest, and offer for your cleansing, accordingly as Moses commanded, for a testimony to them"**.

19. However, so much fame went abroad about him that great multitudes came together to hear, and to be healed by him of their infirmities.

20. And he withdrew himself into the wilderness, and prayed. And it came to pass on a certain day, as he was teaching, that there were Pharisees and doctors of the law sitting by, who had come out of every town of Galilee, and Judaea, and Jerusalem: and the power of the Lord was *present* to heal them.

21. And, behold, men brought in a bed a man who was taken with a palsy: and they sought *means* to bring him in, and to lay *him* before him. And when they could not find a *way* that they might bring him in because of the multitude, they went upon the housetop, and let him down through the tiling in his bed into the midst before Jesus. And when he saw their faith, he said to him, **"Man, your sins are forgiven you"**.

22. And the scribes and the Pharisees began to reason, saying, 'Who is this which speaks these blasphemies?' Who can forgive sins, but God alone?' But when Jesus perceived their thoughts, he answered to them, **"What do you reason in your hearts? Whether is easier, to say, 'your sins be forgiven you; or to say, Rise up and walk'?"** Then he said. **"But, so that you may know that the Son of man has power upon earth to forgive sins,** (he said to the man sick of the palsy,) **"I say to you, Arise, and take up your couch, and go to your house"**.

23. And immediately he rose up before them, and took up that which he lay on, and departed to his own house, glorifying God. And they were all amazed, and they glorified God, and were filled with fear, saying, 'We have seen strange things to day.'
24. And after these things, he went forth, and saw a publican, named Levi, sitting at the receipt of custom: and he said to him, "**Follow me!**" As he left, all rose up, and followed him. And Levi made him a great feast in his own house: and there was a great company of publicans and others that sat down with them. But the scribes and Pharisees murmured against his disciples, saying, 'Why do you eat and drink with publicans and sinners'? And Jesus in reply, said to them, "**They that are whole and need not a physician; but they that are sick are the ones in need.** I came not to call the righteous, but sinners to repentance.**"
25. And they said to him, 'Why do the disciples of John fast often, and make thus, and likewise *the disciples* of the Pharisees; but you eat and drink?' And he said to them, "**Can you make the children of the bride chamber fast, while the bridegroom is with them? But the days will come, when the bridegroom will be taken away from them, and then will they fast in those days.**"
26. And he also related a parable to them; "**No man puts a piece of a new garment upon an old, because, then both the new makes a tear and the piece that was *taken* out of the new agrees not with the old. No man puts new wine into old bottles; else the new wine will burst the bottles, and be spilled, and the bottles will perish. But new wine must be put into new bottles, and both are preserved. No**

man also having drunk old *wine* straightway desires new; for it is said, the old is better."

27. And it came to pass on the second Sabbath after the first, that as he went through the cornfields, his disciples plucked the ears of corn, and ate, rubbing *them* in *their* hands. And certain of the Pharisees said to them, 'Why do you that which is not lawful to do on the Sabbath days'? And Jesus answered them saying, **"Will you not read so much as this, what David did, when himself was hungry along with those who were with him. How he went into the house of God, and took and ate the showbread, and gave it to them that were with him that which it is not lawful to eat except for the priests alone?"** And he said to them, **"The Son of man is Lord commands the Sabbath also."**

28. In addition, it happened on another Sabbath that he entered into the synagogue and taught: and there was a man whose right hand was withered. The scribes and Pharisees watched him, to see whether he would heal on the Sabbath day so that they might find an accusation against him. However, he knew their thoughts, and said to the man who had the withered hand, **"Rise up, and stand forth in the midst"**. And he arose and stood forth. Then said Jesus to them, **"I will ask you one thing; is it lawful on the Sabbath days to do good, or to do evil? To save life, or to destroy** *it***?"**

29. And looking around and about upon them all, he said to the man, **"Stretch forth your hand."** In addition, he did so: and his hand was restored as completely as the other was.

And they were filled with madness; and communed with one another what they might do to Jesus.

30. And it came to pass in those days, that he went out onto a mountain to pray to God, and continued all night.

31. Later, he lifted up his eyes on his disciples, and said to the multitude, "**Blessed *be you* poor: for yours is the kingdom of God. Blessed *are you* that hunger now: for you will be filled. Blessed *are you* that weep now: for you will laugh. Blessed are you, when men will hate you, and when they will separate you *from their company,* and will reproach *you,* and cast out your name as evil, for the Son of man's sake.

32. Rejoice in that day, and leap for joy: for, behold, your reward *is* great in heaven: for in same manner as did their fathers to the prophets. But woe unto you who are rich! For you will receive your consolation. Woe to you who are full! For you will hunger. Woe to you who laugh now! For you will mourn and weep. Woe to you when all men will speak well of you! For so did their fathers do the same to the false prophets.

33. However, I say to you who hear, Love your enemies, and do good to them, which hate you. Bless those who curse you, and pray for them who despitefully use you.

34. And to him that smites you on the *one* cheek offer him the other; and he that takes away your cloak let him *take your* coat also.

35. Give to every man who asks of you, and regarding him who takes away your goods, do not ask them to return them. And as you wish what men should do to you, do you to them likewise. For, if you love those who love you,

what thank will you have? For sinners also love those that love them. And if you do good to them who do good to you, what thank will you have? For sinners also do even the same.

36. And if you lend *to those from* whom you hope to receive, what thank will you? For sinners also lend to sinners, to receive as much in return. But love you your enemies, and do good, and lend, hoping for nothing again; and your reward will be great, and you will be the children of the Highest: for he is kind unto the unthankful and *to* the evil.

37. Be you therefore merciful, as your Father also is merciful. Judge not, and you will not be judged: condemn not, and you will not be condemned: forgive, and you will be forgiven: Give and it will be given unto you. Good measure, pressed down, and shaken together, and running over, will men give into your bosom. For with the same measure that you give out, it will be measured out to you again.

38. And he spoke a parable to them, "Can the blind lead the blind? Will they not both fall into the ditch? The disciple is not above his master: but everyone that is perfect will be as his master.

39. Why point out the mote that is in your brother's eye, but not perceive the beam that is in your own eye? Either how can you say to your brother, Brother, let me pull out the mote that is in your eye, when you yourself do not see the beam that is in your own eye? You hypocrite! First cast out the beam out of your own eye, and then will you see clearly to pull out the mote that is in your brother's eye.

40. For a good tree does not brings forth corrupt fruit; neither does a corrupt tree bring forth good fruit. For every tree is known by its own fruit. Because from thorns men do not gather figs, nor from a bramble bush do they gather grapes. A good man out of the good treasure of his heart brings forth that which is good; and an evil man out of the evil treasure of his heart brings forth that which is evil: for from the abundance of the heart his mouth speaks.

41. And why do you call out to me, 'Lord, Lord' and do not do the things that I say? Whoever comes to me, and hears my sayings, and does them, I will tell you who he is like. He is like a man which built an house, and dug deep, and laid the foundation on a rock and when the flood arose, the stream beat vehemently upon that house, and could not shake it: for it was founded upon a rock. But he that hears, and does not do the things I say, is like a man that built a house without a foundation in the earth; against which the stream did beat vehemently, and immediately it fell; and the ruin of that house was great."

42. Now when he had ended all his sayings in the audience of the people, he entered into Capernaum. And a certain Roman Centurion's servant, who was dear to him, was sick and ready to die. And when he heard of Jesus, he sent to him the elders of the Jews, beseeching him that he would come and heal his servant. And when they came to Jesus, they asked him instantly, saying, that he (the Centurion) was concerned about who Jesus would be doing this for. For he loves our nation and he has built us a synagogue.

43. Then Jesus went with them. When he was not far from the house, the Centurion sent friends to him, saying to him, 'Lord, trouble not yourself: for I am not concerned that you should enter under my roof: neither did I think it necessary to come to you. Just say the word, and my servant will be healed. For I also am a man set under authority, having under me soldiers, and I say to one, Go, and he goes; and to another, Come, and he comes; and to my servant, Do this, and he does it.'
44. When Jesus heard these things, he marveled at him, and turned him about, and said to the people that followed him, "**I say to you, I have not found so great faith, no, not in all of Israel.**" When the messengers, returned to the Centurions' house, they found the servant that had been sick had been healed.
45. And it came to pass the day after, that he went into a city called Nain and many of his disciples went with him, and many people. Now when he came near to the gate of the city, behold, there was a dead man carried out, the only son of his mother, and she was a widow: and many people from the city were with her. When the Lord saw her, he had compassion on her, and said to her, "**Weep not**".
46. He approached and touched the bier: and they that carried *him* stood still. And he said, "**Young man, I say to you, Arise!**" And he that was dead sat up, and began to speak. And he was returned to his mother. And there came a fear upon all there. And they glorified God, saying, that a great prophet is risen up among us and that God had visited his people. This rumor about him went forth throughout all Judaea, and throughout all the region round about.

47. And the disciples of John the Baptist told John about all these things.
48. And John called to him two of his disciples and sent them to Jesus, asking, 'Are you he that should come, or do we look for another'? When the men came to him, they said, 'John the Baptist has sent us to you, asking, 'Are you He that should come, or should we look for another?' And in that same hour he cured many of their infirmities and plagues, drove out evil spirits, and to many that were blind he gave sight. Then Jesus answered and said to them, "**Go your way, and tell John what things you have seen and heard. How the blind see, the lame walk, the lepers are cleansed, the deaf hear, the dead are raised, and to the gospel is preached to the poor. And blessed is** *he,* **whoever will not be offended by me.**"
49. And when the messengers of John had left, he began to speak to the people concerning John, "**What did you go out into the wilderness to see? A reed shaken with the wind? What did you go out to see? A man clothed in soft fine clothes? Behold, they who are gorgeously appareled and live delicately are in kings courts. What did you go out to see? A prophet? Yes, I say to you, and much more than a prophet.**
50. **This is** *he,* **of whom it is written, 'Behold, I send my messenger before your face, who will prepare your way before you.' For I say to you, among those that are born of women there is not a greater prophet than John the Baptist. However, he that is least in the kingdom of God is greater than John is.**

51. And all the people that heard *him,* and even the publicans, justified with God, being baptized with the baptism of John. But the Pharisees and lawyers rejected the counsel of God against themselves, being not baptized.

52. And the Lord said, **"To what then will I liken the men of this generation? What are they like? They are like children sitting in the marketplace, and calling one to another, and saying, we have played music to you, and you have not danced; we have mourned to you, and you have not wept. For John the Baptist came neither eating bread nor drinking wine; and you say He was a devil. The Son of man has come eating and drinking and you say, Behold a gluttonous man, and a winebibber, a friend of publicans and sinners! But wisdom is justified of all her children.**

53. And one of the Pharisees desired that he would eat with him. And he went into the Pharisee's house, and sat down to meat. And, behold, there was a woman in the city, who was a sinner, and when she knew that *Jesus* sat at meat in the Pharisee's house, brought an alabaster box of ointment. She stood at his feet behind *him* weeping and began to wash his feet with tears and wiped *them* with the hair of her head, and kissed his feet, and anointed *them* with the ointment.

54. Now when the Pharisee who had invited him saw *it,* he spoke within himself, saying, 'This man, if he were a prophet, would have known who and what manner of woman *this is* that touched him: for she is a sinner'. And Jesus in answer said to him, **"Simon, I have something to say to you."** And he said, 'Master, speak on'. **"There was a**

certain creditor who had two debtors: the one owed five hundred pence, and the other fifty. And when they had nothing to pay, he frankly forgave them both."

55. "**Tell me therefore, which of these men will love him most?** Simon answered and said, 'I suppose that *he*, to whom he forgave most'. And Jesus said to him, "**You have rightly judged.**" And he turned to the woman, and said to Simon, "**See this woman? I entered into your house; you gave me no water for my feet: but she has washed my feet with tears, and wiped *them* with the hairs of her head. You gave me no kiss: but this woman, since the time I came in, has not ceased to kiss my feet. You did not anoint my head with oil; but this woman has anointed my feet with ointment. Therefore, I say to you, her sins, which are many, are forgiven, for she loved much: but for the person for whom little is forgiven, *that same* person is also loved little.**" And he said to her, "**Your sins are forgiven**". And they who sat at dinner with him began to say within themselves, 'Who is this person who also forgives sins?' And he said to the woman, "**Your faith has saved you; go in peace.**"

56. And it came to pass afterward, that he went throughout every city and village. Preaching and showing the glad tidings of the kingdom of God: and the twelve *were* with him, And a certain women, who had been healed of evil spirits and infirmities, Mary called Magdalene, out of whom seven devils were banished, And Joanna the wife of Chuza Herod's steward, and Susanna, and many others, who ministered to him from their substance.

57. And when many people had gathered together and came to him out of every city, he spoke a parable: **"A farmer went out to sow his seed: and as he sowed, some fell by the way side; and it was trodden down, and the fowls of the air devoured it. And some fell upon a rock; and as soon as it sprung up, it withered away, because it lacked moisture. And some fell among thorns; and the thorns sprang up with it, and choked it. And others fell upon good ground, and sprang up, and bore fruit a hundredfold."**

58. And when he had said these things, he cried, **"He that has ears to hear, let him hear!"** And his disciples inquired of him, saying, 'What might this parable be?' And he said, **"Unto you it is given to know the mysteries of the kingdom of God: but to others it is given in parables; that seeing they might not see and hearing they might not understand. Now the parable is this: The seed is the word of God. Those that fell by the way side are they that hear, and then the devil comes, and takes away the word out of their hearts, lest they should believe and be saved.**

59. Those sown on the rock *are they,* which, when they hear, receive the word with joy, and these there is no root, who for a while believe, but in time of temptation fall away.

60. And those seeds that fell among thorns are they, who, when they hear, go forth, and are choked with cares and riches and pleasures of *this* life, and bring no fruit to perfection.

61. However, those seeds that fell on the good ground are they, which in an honest and good heart, having heard the word, keep *it,* and bring forth fruit with patience.

62. No man, when he has lighted a candle, covers it with a vessel, or puts *it* under a bed. But he sets *it* on a candlestick, so that they who enter in may see the light. For nothing is secret, that will not be made manifest. Nor is there anything hidden, that will not be known and come out. Take heed therefore, how you hear: for whoever has, to him it will be given; and whoever has not, from him it will be taken, even that which he already has.

63. Then *his* mother and his brothers came to him, and could not come near him because of the press of people. And it was told to him *by certain* people who said, 'Your mother and your brothers stand outside, desiring to see you.' And he answered and said to them, "**My mother and my brothers are these who hear the word of God, and do it.**"

64. Now it came to pass on a certain day, that he went onto a ship with his disciples: and he said to them, "**Let us go over to the other side of the Sea**". And they launched forth. However, as they sailed he fell asleep: and there came down a storm of wind on the lake; and they were flooded *with water,* and were in jeopardy. And they came to him, and awoke him, saying, 'Master, master, we perish.' Then he arose, and rebuked the wind and the raging of the water: and they ceased, and there was calm. And he said to them, "**Where is your faith?**" And they being afraid, wondered, saying one to another, 'What manner of man is this! For he commands even the winds and water, and they obey him.'

65. And they arrived at the country of the Gadarenes, which is over against Galilee. And when he landed, he met a certain

man who came out of the city, who had had devils for a long time, who wore no clothes, and neither lived in *any* house, but in the tombs. When he saw Jesus, he cried out, and fell down before him, and with a loud voice said, 'What have I to do with you, Jesus, *you* Son of God most high? I beseech you, do not torment me.' (For Jesus had commanded the unclean spirit to come out of the man. For oftentimes, it had caught him and he was kept bound with chains and in fetters; and he had often broken the bands, and was driven by the spirits into the wilderness.)

66. Jesus asked him, "**What is your name?**" And he answered,' Legion', because many devils had entered into him. And they pleaded with him that he would not command them to go out into the waters. There was there a herd of many swine feeding on the mountain, and they asked him if he would allow them to enter into them. He allowed them to do so and then the devils left the man, and entered into the swine, and the herd ran violently down a steep place into the lake and drowned.

67. When the swineherds saw what was done to the pigs, they fled, and went and told *it* in the city and in the country. Then the people went out to see what was done; and came to Jesus, and found the man, out of whom the devils had been driven, sitting at the feet of Jesus, clothed, and in his right mind. They were afraid because they had been told of the means that the man who was possessed of the devils was healed.

68. Then the whole multitude of the country of the Gadarenes round about asked him to depart from them; for they were taken with great fear: and he went up onto the ship, and

made preparations to return. But the man out of whom the devils were departed asked him that he might stay with him, but Jesus sent him away, saying, **"Return to your own house, and show how great things God has done unto you."** And the man went his way, and published throughout the whole city what great things Jesus had done for him. And it came to pass, that, when Jesus returned, the people gladly received him: for they were all waiting for him.

69. And a woman having an issue of blood for twelve years, who had spent all her living upon physicians, who could not be healed, who came up behind him, and touched the border of his garment: and immediately her issue of blood stopped. And Jesus said, **"Who touched me?"** When all denied it, Peter and they that were with him said, 'Master, the multitude throng you and press *you,* and you say, **who touched me?'** And Jesus said, **"Someone has touched me: for I perceive that virtue is gone out of me."**

70. And when the woman saw that she could not hide, she came trembling, and falling down before him, she declared to him before all the people the reason she had touched him and how she was healed immediately. He said to her, **"Daughter, be of good comfort: your faith has made you whole; go in peace."**

71. While he thus spoke, there came one from the ruler of the synagogue's *house,* those about said to him, 'Your master's daughter is dead; do not trouble the Master'. However, when Jesus heard *it,* he answered him, saying, **"Fear not: believe only, and she will be made whole."** And when he came into the house, he allowed no man to go in with him,

except Peter, and James, and John, and the father and the mother of the maiden. And all wept, and bewailed her: but he said, "**Weep not; she is not dead, but sleeps**".

72. And they laughed at him in scorn, knowing that she was dead. And he put them all out, and took her by the hand, and called, saying, "**Child, arise!**" And her spirit came again, and she arose straightway: and he commanded them to give her food. Her parents were astonished: but he charged them that they should tell no man what was done.

73. Then he called his twelve disciples together, and gave them power and authority over all devils to cure diseases. And he sent them to preach the kingdom of God, and to heal the sick. And he said to them, "**Take nothing for *your* journey, neither staves, nor script, neither bread, neither money; neither have two coats apiece. And whatever house you enter into, stay there, and then depart. And whoever will not receive you, when you go out of that city, shake off the very dust from your feet for a testimony against them.**" And they departed, and went through the towns, preaching the gospel, and healing everywhere.

74. Now Herod the King heard of all that was done by Jesus: and he was perplexed, because that it was said of some, that John had risen from the dead; And of some, that Elias had appeared; and of others, that one of the old prophets was risen again. Herod said, 'I have beheaded John: but who is this of whom I hear such things'? And he desired to see him.

75. And the apostles, when they returned, told Jesus all that they had done. And he took them and went aside privately into a desert place belonging to the city called Bethsaida. And the people, when they knew *it,* followed him: and he received them, and spoke to them of the kingdom of God, and healed them that had need of healing.
76. And when the day began to wear away, then came the twelve, and said to him, 'Send the multitude away, so that they may go into the towns and country round about, and lodge, and get victuals: for we are here in a desert place'. But he replied to them, **"You give them something to eat."** In addition, they said, 'We have no more than five loaves and two fishes; unless we should go and buy meat for all these people'. For there were about five thousand.'
77. And Jesus said to his disciples; **"Make them sit down by fifties in a company."** And they did so, and made the crowd sit down. Then he took the five loaves and the two fishes, and looking up to heaven, he blessed them, and broke the bread, and gave it to the disciples to set before the multitude. And they ate, and were all filled: and there were twelve baskets of fragments that remained.
78. And it came to pass, as he was alone praying, his disciples were with him: and he asked them, saying, **"Who do the people say that I am?"** They answering said, John the Baptist; but some *say,* Elias; and others *say,* that one of the old prophets has risen again. He asked them again, **"But who do you say that I am?"** Peter answered said, 'The Christ of God'. And he straightly charged them, and commanded *them* to tell no man that thing; saying, **"The Son of Man must suffer many things, and be rejected of**

the elders and chief priests and scribes, and be slain, and be raised on the third day".

79. Then he said to all of *them*, "**If any *man* will come after me, let him deny himself, and take up his cross daily, and follow me. For whoever will save his life will lose it: but whoever will lose his life for my sake, the same will save it. For what is a man advantaged, if he gains the whole world, and loses himself, or be cast away? For whoever will be ashamed of me and of my words, of him will the Son of Man be ashamed when he comes in his own glory, and *in his* Father's glory, and of the glory of the holy angels. But I tell you truly, there are some standing here, who will not taste of death, till they see the kingdom of God."**

80. And it came to pass, that on the next day, when they came down from the hill, many people met him. And, behold, a man from the company cried out, saying, 'Master, I beseech you, look at my son: for he is my only child. A spirit takes the boy, and he suddenly cries out; and it tears him and he foams at the mouth, and it bruises him and hardly departs from him. I asked your disciples to cast him out; and they could not.'

81. Jesus answered, "**Oh, faithless and perverse generation, how long will I be with you, and suffer you? Bring your son here.**" And as he was coming, the devil threw the young boy down, and tore at *him*. Jesus rebuked the unclean spirit, and healed the child, and delivered him again to his father.

82. They were all amazed at the mighty power of God. But while they wondered at all things that Jesus did, he said to

his disciples, "**Let these sayings sink down into your ears: for the Son of man will be delivered into the hands of men.**" However, they did not understand this saying, and it was hid from them, so that they did not perceive it: and they feared to ask him about this saying.

83. Then there arose a reasoning among them about who among them would be the greatest. And Jesus, perceiving the thought of their hearts, took a child, and set him by his side, and said to them, "**Whoever will receive this child in my name receives me: and whoever receives me receives him that sent me: for he that is least among you all, the same will be the greatest.**"

84. And John answered and said, 'Master, we saw one casting out devils in your name; and we forbad him, because he does not follow us.' And Jesus said to him**, "Do not forbid *him*: for he that is not against us is with us."**

85. And it came to pass, when the time came that he should be received up into heaven, he steadfastly set his face to go to Jerusalem, and he sent his messengers before him: and they went, and entered into a village of the Samaritans, to make ready for him. But they would not receive him, because his face was as though he would go to Jerusalem.

86. And when his disciples James and John saw *this,* they said, 'Lord, will it that we command fire to come down from heaven, and consume them, even as Elias did?' But he turned, and rebuked them, and said, "**You know not what manner of spirit you are of. For the Son of man has not come to destroy men's lives, but to save *them.* And they went to another village.**"

87. And it came to pass, that, as they went in the way, a certain *man* said to him, "Lord, I will follow you wherever you go.' And Jesus said to him, "**Foxes have holes, and birds of the air** *have* **nests; but the Son of man has nowhere to lay** *his* **head**". And he said to another, "**Follow me!**" But the man said, 'Lord, allow me first to go and bury my father'. Jesus said to him, "**Let the dead bury their dead: and go and preach the kingdom of God.**" And another also said, 'Lord, I will follow you; but let me first go bid them farewell, who are at home at my house.' And Jesus said to him, "**No man, having put his hand to the plough, and looking back, is fit for the kingdom of God.**"

88. After these things the Lord appointed other seventy also, and sent them two and two before his face into every city and place, where he himself might come. '**Therefore,**" said he to them, "**The harvest truly** *is* **great, but the laborers** *are* **few: pray you therefore the Lord of the harvest, that he would send forth laborers into his harvest. Go your ways: behold, I send you forth as lambs among wolves. Carry neither purse, nor script, nor shoes: and salute no man by the way. And into whatever house you enter, first say, Peace** *be* **unto this house. And if the son of peace is there, your peace will rest upon it: if not, it will return to you again. And in the same house remain, eating and drinking such things as they give: for the laborer is worrying of his hire.**

89. Do not go from house to house. And into whatever city you enter, and they receive you, eat such things as are set before you: And heal the sick that are therein, and say to them, The kingdom of God is come soon to you. But into whatsoever city you enter, and they do not receive you, go your ways out into the streets of the same city, and say, 'Even the very dust of your city, which sticks on us, we do wipe off against you.'

90. Be sure of this, that the kingdom of God is come soon unto you. I say to you, that it will be more tolerable in that day for Sodom, than for that city. Woe unto you, Chorazin! woe unto you, Bethsaida! for if the mighty works had been done in Tyre and Sidon, which have been done in you, they had a great while ago repented, sitting in sackcloth and ashes. But it will be more tolerable for Tyre and Sidon at the judgment, than for you. And you, Capernaum, which is exalted to heaven, will be thrust down to hell. He that hears you, hears me; and he that despises you, despises me; and he that despises, me despises him that sent me."

91. And the seventy returned again with joy, saying, Lord, even the devils are subject to us through your name. And he said to them, "I beheld Satan as lightning falling from heaven. Behold, I give to you power to tread on serpents and scorpions, and power over all of the enemy: and nothing will by any means hurt you. Even so, do not rejoice that the spirits are subject to you; but rather rejoice, because your names are written in heaven."

92. In that hour Jesus rejoiced in spirit, and said, "I thank you, O Father, Lord of heaven and earth, that you have hid these things from the wise and prudent, and have revealed them unto babes: even so, Father; for so it seemed good in your sight. All things are delivered to me of my Father: and no man knows who the Son is, but the

Father; and who the Father is, but the Son, and *he* to whom the Son will reveal *him.*"

93. And he turned to his disciples, and said privately, "**Blessed are the eyes which see the things that you see: For I tell you, that many prophets and kings have desired to see those things which you see, and will not seen them; and to hear those things which you hear, and will not hear them.**"

94. And, behold, a certain lawyer stood up, and tempted him, saying, 'Master, 'What will I do to inherit eternal life?' He said to him, "**What is written in the law? how do you read it?**" And the man answered, 'You must love the Lord your God with all your heart, and with all your soul, and with all your strength, and with all your mind; and your neighbor as yourself'. And Jesus told him, "**You have answered correctly: do this, and you will live.**"

95. But he, wanting to justify himself, said to Jesus, 'And who is my neighbor'? And Jesus answered and said, "**A certain *man* went down from Jerusalem to Jericho, and fell among thieves, who stripped him of his clothes, and wounded *him,* and departed, leaving *him* half dead. And by chance there came down a certain priest that way: and when he saw him, he passed by on the other side. And likewise, a Levite, when he came to the place, looked *on him,* and passed by on the other side.**

96. **But a certain Samaritan, as he journeyed, came where he was: and when he saw him, he had compassion *on him,* And went to *him,* and bound up his wounds, pouring in oil and wine, and set him on his own beast, and brought him to an inn, and took care of him. And on the morrow when**

he departed, he took out two pence, and gave *them* to the host, and said to him, 'Take care of him; and whatever you spend more, when I come again, I will repay you.' Now, which of these three, do you think was a neighbor to him that fell among the thieves? And the man said, 'He that showed mercy on him.' Then said Jesus to him, "**Go, and do likewise**".

97. Now it came to pass, as they went, that he entered into a certain village: and a certain woman named Mareha received him into her house. And she had a sister called Mary, who also sat at Jesus' feet, and heard his word. But Mareha was cumbered about much serving, and came to him, and said, 'Lord, do you not care that my sister has left me to serve alone? Tell her therefore that she help me'. And Jesus answered and said to her, "**Mareha, Mareha, you are careful and troubled about many things: But one thing is needful: and Mary has chosen that good part, which will not be taken away from her.**"

98. And it came to pass, that as he was praying in a certain place, when he ceased, one of his disciples said to him, 'Lord, teach us to pray, as John also taught his disciples.' And he said to them, When you pray, say this,

99. "<u>**Our Father which art in heaven, Hallowed be your name. Thy kingdom come. Thy will be done, as in heaven, so in earth. Give us day by day our daily bread and forgive us our sins; for we also forgive every one that is indebted to us. And lead us not into temptation; but deliver us from evil.**</u>"

100. And he said to them, "**Which of you has a friend, and would go to him at midnight, and say to him, 'Friend, lend

me three loaves; For a friend of mine on his journey has come to see me, and I have nothing to set before him? Suppose that he from within answers and says, 'Don't bother me: the door is now shut, and my children are with me in bed; I cannot rise and give you anything.'"

101. I say to you, Even though he does not want rise and give the loaves to him, but, because he is his friend, because of his importunity he will rise and give him as many loaves as he needs. And I say to you, Ask, and it will be given you; Seek, and you will find; Knock, and it will be opened unto you. For everyone that asks he will receive, and he that seeks will find; and to him that knocks it will be opened.

102. If a son will asks for bread from any of you that is a father, will he give him a stone? Or if *he ask* for a fish, will he give him a serpent? Or if he asks for an egg, will he offer him a scorpion? If you then, being evil, know how to give good gifts to your children: how much more will *your* heavenly Father know how to give the Holy Spirit to those that ask him?"

103. And he was casting out a devil, and it was dumbness. And it came to pass, when the devil was gone out, the dumb one spoke; and the people wondered. But some of them said, He casts out devils through Beelzebub the chief of the devils. And others, tempting *him,* sought of him a sign from heaven. But he, knowing their thoughts, said to them, **"Every kingdom divided against itself is brought to desolation; and a house *divided* against a house falls. If Satan also is divided against himself, how will his kingdom stand? But you say that I cast out devils through**

Beelzebub. If I cast out by Beelzebub devils, by whom do your sons cast *them* out? therefore will they be your judges. But if I, with the finger of God, cast out devils, no doubt the kingdom of God is come upon you.

104. **When a strong armed man keeps his palace, his goods are in peace: But when one stronger than he comes upon him, and overcomes him, he takes from him all of his armor in which he trusted, and divides his spoils. He that is not with me is against me: and he that gathers not with me scatters.**

105. **When the unclean spirit leaves out of a man, it walks through dry places, seeking rest; and finding none, it says, I will return to the house where I came from. And when he comes, he finds *it* swept and garnished. Then he goes, and takes *with him* seven other spirits more wicked than himself; and they enter in to a man, and dwell there: and the last *state* of that man is worse than the first.**

106. And it came to pass, as he spoke these things, a certain woman of the company lifted up her voice, and said to him, 'Blessed is the womb that bore you, and the teats which you have sucked'. "**But He said, Rather, blessed *are* they that hear the word of God, and keep it.**"

107. And when the people were gathered thick together, he said, "**This is an evil generation: they seek a sign; and there will no sign be given it, but the sign of Jonas the prophet. For as Jonas was a sign unto the Ninevites, so will also the Son of Man be to this generation. The queen of Sheba will rise up in the judgment with the men of this generation, and condemn them: for she came from the**

utmost parts of the earth to hear the wisdom of Solomon; and, behold, one greater than Solomon is here.

108. The men of Nineve will rise up in the judgment against this generation, and will condemn it: for they repented at the preaching of Jonas; and, behold, a greater than Jonas *is* here. No man, when he has lighted a candle, puts *it* in a secret place, neither under a bushel, but on a candlestick, so that they who enter may see the light. The light of the body is the eye. Therefore, when your eye is single, your whole body also is full of light; but when *your eye* is evil, your body also *is* full of darkness. Take heed therefore that the light which is in you is not that of darkness. If your whole body therefore *is* full of light, having no part dark, the whole will be full of light, as when the bright shining of a candle gives light."

109. And as he spoke, a certain Pharisee besought him to dine with him: and he went in, and sat down to meat. And when the Pharisee saw *it,* he marveled that he had not first washed his hands before dinner. And the Lord said to him, "Now, you Pharisees make clean the outside of the cup and the platter; but your inward part is full of ravening and wickedness. *You* fools, did not he that made that which is without make that which is within also? Rather give alms of such things as you will; and, behold, all things are clean unto you. But woe unto you, Pharisees! For you tithe mint, rue, and all manner of herbs, and pass over judgment and the love of God: these things you ought to do well, and not to leave the other undone. Woe unto you, Pharisees! For you love the uppermost seats in the synagogues, and greetings in the markets. Woe unto you,

scribes and Pharisees, hypocrites! For you are as graves which are hidden, and the men that walk over *them* are not aware *of them.*

110. Then one of the lawyers answered, and said to him, 'Master, thus saying you reproach us also'. And he said, **"Woe unto you also, *you* lawyers! for you load men with burdens grievous to be borne, and you yourselves do not touch the burdens with even one of your fingers. Woe unto you! For you build the sepulchers of the prophets, and your fathers killed them. Truly, you bear witness that you allowed the deeds of your fathers: for they indeed killed them, and you built their sepulchers.**

111. **Therefore the wisdom of God also said, 'I will send them prophets and apostles, and *some* of them they will slay and persecute so that the blood of all the prophets, which was shed from the foundation of the world, may be required of this generation. From the blood of Abel unto the blood of Zacharias, who perished between the altar and the temple: Verily, I say to you, much will be required of this generation. Woe unto you, lawyers! For you have taken away the key of knowledge: you did not enter in yourselves, and you hindered those who were entering."**

112. And as he said these things to them, the scribes and the Pharisees began to urge *him* vehemently, and to provoke him to speak of many things: Laying wait for him, and seeking to catch something out of his mouth, that they might accuse him of.

113. In the mean time, there gathered together an innumerable multitude of people, so many that they stepped one upon another. He began to say to his disciples first of all,

"Beware of the leaven of the Pharisees, which is hypocrisy. For there is nothing covered, that will not be revealed; neither hid, that will not be known. Therefore, whatever you have spoken in darkness will be heard in the light; and that which you have whispered in the ear in closets will be proclaimed upon the housetops.

114. And I say unto you my friends, Be not afraid of them that kill the body, and after that there is no more that they can do. Nevertheless, I will forewarn you whom you should fear: Fear him, which after he has killed has power to cast into hell; Thus, I say to you, Fear him. Are not five sparrows sold for two farthings, and not one of them is forgotten before God? Even the very hairs of your head are all numbered. Fear not therefore: you are of more value than many sparrows.

115. Also I say unto you, Whoever will confess me before men, for him will the Son of Man also confess before the angels of God: But he that denies me before men will be denied before the angels of God. And whoever will speak a word against the Son of Man, it will be forgiven him: but to him that blasphemes against the Holy Ghost it will not be forgiven. And when they bring you into the synagogues, and *before* magistrates, and powers that be, take no thought how or what thing you will answer, or what you will say: For the Holy Ghost will teach you in the same hour what you ought to say."

116. And one of the company said to him, 'Rabbi, speak to my brother, so that he will divide the inheritance with me'. And he said to him, "**Who made me a judge or a divider over you?**" And Jesus continued, "**Take heed, and beware**

of covetousness: for a man's life consists not in the abundance of the things that he possesses."

117. And he spoke a parable to them, saying, "**The ground of a certain rich man brought forth plentifully: And he thought to himself, saying, what will I do, because I have no room where to store my fruits? And he said, This will I do: I will pull down my barns, and build a greater one; and there will I hold all my fruits and my goods. And I will say to my soul, Soul, you have much goods laid up for many years; take your ease, eat, drink,** *and* **be merry. But God said to him, '*You* fool, this night your soul will be required of you: then who will those things belong to, which you have provided?'** He that lays up treasure for himself on earth is not rich toward God."

118. And he said to his disciples, "**Therefore I say to you, Take no thought for your life, what you will eat; neither for the body, what you will put on. Life is more than food, and the body** *is more* **than clothes. Consider the ravens, for they neither sow nor do they reap. Neither do they have a storehouse or a barn, and God feeds them: How much more are you better than the birds?**

119. **And which of you by taking thought can add to his stature one inch? If then, you are not able to do that thing which is least, why take you thought for the rest? Consider the lilies of the field and how they grow: they do not toil, they do not spin. Thus, I say to you, that Solomon in all his glory was not arrayed like one of these. If then God so clothed the grass, which is to day in the field, and tomorrow is cast into the oven; how much more will he clothe you, O you of little faith! Seek not what you will

eat, or what you will drink, neither be of doubtful mind. For all these things do the nations of the world seek after: and your Father knows that you will need these things.

120. Rather, seek the kingdom of God; and all these things will be added unto you. Fear not, little flock, for it is your Father's good pleasure to give you the kingdom. Sell what you will, and give alms; provide yourselves bags which do not get old, a treasure in the heavens that fails not, where no thief approaches, neither moths corrupt. For where your treasure is, there will your heart be also. Let your loins be girded about, and your lights burning.

121. And you yourselves should be like servants that wait for their lord, when he will return from the wedding, so that when he comes and knocks, they may open the door for him immediately. Blessed *are* those servants, whom the lord, when he comes' will find watching:

122. Verily, I say to you, that he will gird himself, and make them to sit down to meat, and will come forth and serve them. Moreover, if he will come in the second watch, or come in the third watch, and find them watching, blessed are those servants. And know this, that if the good man of the house had known what hour the thief would come, he would have watched, and not have allowed his house to be broken into. Therefore, be ready also: for the Son of man comes at an hour when you think not."

123. Then Peter said to him, 'Lord, explain this parable to us, or even to all?' And the Lord said, "**Who then is that faithful and wise servant, who his lord will make ruler over his household, and give** *them their* **portion of meat in due season? Blessed** *is* **that servant, who when his lord comes**

will be found so faithful. Truly, I say to you, that he will make him ruler over all that he has.

124. But and if that servant says in his heart, My lord is late in coming; and starts to beat the menservants and maidens, and to eat and drink, and to be drunken. The lord of that servant will come in a day when he is not looking for *him*, and at an hour when he is not aware, will cut him asunder, and will appoint him his portion with the unbelievers. And that servant, who knew his lord's will, and did not prepare himself, and neither did according to His will, will be beaten with many *straps*. But he that knew not, and did commit things worrying about straps, will be beaten with few *straps*. For unto whoever much is given, of him much will be required: and to him who has been given much, of him they will ask more.

125. I am come to send fire on the earth, and what have I if it is already kindled? However, I still have a baptism to be baptized with, and how I am constrained until it is accomplished! Suppose that I have come to give peace on earth? I will tell you, No; but rather division on earth: For from henceforth there will be five in one house divided, three against two, and two against three. The father will be divided against the son, and the son against the father; the mother against the daughter, and the daughter against the mother; the mother-in-law against her daughter-in-law, and the daughter-in-law against her mother-in-law."

126. And he said to the people, "When you see a cloud rise out of the west, straightway you say, there comes a shower; and so it is. And when *you see* the south wind blow, you

say, there will be heat; and it comes to pass. *You hypocrites!* You can discern the face of the sky and of the earth. But how is it that you cannot discern this time? This is why, even about yourselves; you cannot judge what is right?

127. When you go with your adversary to the magistrate, *as you are* in the wrong, give diligence that you may be delivered from him; lest he bring you before the judge, and the judge deliver you to the officer, and the officer cast you into prison. I tell you, you will not depart from here, until you have paid the very last mite."

128. There were present at that season some who told him of the Galileans, whose blood Pilate had mingled with their sacrifices. And Jesus answered them, "**Suppose that these Galileans were sinners above all the Galileans, because they allowed such things? I tell you, No: but, except you repent, you will all likewise perish. Or those eighteen, upon whom the tower in Siloam fell and slew them, do you think that they were sinners above all men that dwelt in Jerusalem? I tell you, No: but, except you repent, you will all likewise perish."**

129. He spoke this parable also; "**A certain *man* had a fig tree planted in his vineyard; and he came and sought fruit upon it, and found none. Then he said unto the dresser of his vineyard, 'Behold, these three years I come seeking fruit on this fig tree, and find none: cut it down; why waste the ground with it?' And the gardener answering and said to him, 'Lord, let it alone this year also, till I dig about it, and dung *it:* And if it bears fruit, *well:* and if not, *then* after that you should cut it down.'"**

130. And as he was teaching in one of the synagogues on the Sabbath. Behold, there was a woman who had a spirit of infirmity eighteen years, and was bowed over, and could in no wise lift up *herself*. When Jesus saw her, he called *her to him*, and said to her, "**Woman, you are free from your infirmity.**" And he laid his hands on her: and immediately she was made straight, and glorified God.

131. Then the ruler of the synagogue answered with indignation, because Jesus had healed on the Sabbath day, and he said to the people. 'There are six days in which men ought to work on. Therefore come on those days and be healed, but not on the Sabbath day.' The Lord then answered him and said, "***You*** **hypocrite! Does not each one of you on the Sabbath let his ox or *his* ass out of the stall, and lead *him* away to watering? And ought not this woman, being a daughter of Abraham, whom Satan has bound, lo, these eighteen years, be released from this bond on the Sabbath day?**" When he had said these things, all his adversaries were ashamed: and all the people rejoiced for all the glorious things that he did.

132. Then said he, "**Unto what is the kingdom of God like? Moreover, to what will I compare it? It is like a grain of mustard seed, which a man took, and cast into his garden; and it grew, and turned into a great tree; and the fowls of the air lodged in its branches.**" Again he said, "**What will I liken the kingdom of God? It is like leaven, which a woman took and hid in three measures of meal, until the whole loaf lifted.**"

133. And he went through the cities and villages, teaching, and journeying toward Jerusalem. Then one man said to him, 'Lord, are there only a few that will be saved'?

134. And he said to them, **"Strive to enter in at the strait gate: for many, will seek to enter and will not be able. Once the master of the house has risen and has shut the door and you begin to stand outside and knock at the door, saying, 'Lord, Lord, open unto us'. He will answer and say to you, I do not know who you are.**

135. **Then will you begin to say, 'We have eaten and drank in your presence, and you have taught in our streets. But he will say, I tell you, I do not know who you are; depart from me, all *you* workers of iniquity. There will be weeping and gnashing of teeth, when you will see Abraham, and Isaac, and Jacob, and all the prophets, in the kingdom of God, and you *yourselves* will be thrust out.**

136. **And they will come from the east, and *from* the west, and from the north, and *from* the south, and will sit down in the kingdom of God. And, behold, the ones that are last will be first, and the first will be last."**

137. That same day there came certain of the Pharisees, and said to him, 'Go away, and depart from here! For Herod will kill you.' And Jesus said to them, **"Go and tell that fox, Behold, I cast out devils, and I will do cures today and tomorrow, and the third *day* I will be perfected. Nevertheless, I must walk today, and tomorrow, and the *day* following: for it cannot be that a prophet should perish outside of Jerusalem. O, Jerusalem, Jerusalem, you who kills the prophets, and stones them that are sent**

unto you; how often I would have gathered your children together, as a hen gathers her brood under *her* wings, and you Jerusalem, would not do right by them! Behold, your house will be left desolate: and verily, I say unto you, you will not see me, until *the time* comes when you will say, 'Blessed *is* he that comes in the name of the Lord.'

138. And it came to pass, as he went into the house of one of the chief Pharisees to eat bread on the Sabbath day, that they watched him. And, behold, there was a certain man before him who had the dropsy. And Jesus spoke to the lawyers and Pharisees, saying, **"Is it lawful to heal on the Sabbath day?"** And they held their peace. And he touched the man and healed him, and let him go. And answered them, saying, **"Which of you will help an ass or an ox fallen into a pit, and will not straightway pull him out on the Sabbath day?"** Again, they did not have an answer for him about these things.

139. when he noticed who chose out the best rooms, he put forth a parable to those who were there. Saying to them, **"When you are invited by any *man* to a wedding, do not sit down in the highest room; unless a more honorable man than you be invited also; And he that invited you and him to come says to you, give this man your place; and you begin with shame to take the lowest room. But when you are bidden, go and sit down in the lowest room so that when he that asked you to come may say to you, Friend, go up higher, then you will worship in the presence of those who sit to eat with you. For whoever**

exalts himself will be humbled; and he that humbles himself will be exalted."

140. Then he continued, "**When you make a dinner or a supper, don't call your friends, or your brothers, or your kinsmen, or** *your* **rich neighbors; lest they also invite you back to their places, as compensation. But when you make a feast, call the poor, the maimed, the lame, and the blind: And you will be blessed; for they cannot compensate you: for you will be compensated at the resurrection of the just."**

141. And when one of them that sat at meat with him heard these things, he said to him, 'Blessed *is* he that will eat bread in the kingdom of God.' Then Jesus replied to him, **"A certain man made a great supper, and asked many: And sent his servant at supper time to say to them who were invited, Come; for all things are now ready. Then they all, with one** *consent,* **began to make excuses. The first said to him, 'I have bought a piece of ground, and I need go and see it: I pray you will excuse me.' And another said, 'I have bought five yoke of oxen, and I must go to prove them: I pray you will let me be excused.' And another said, 'I have just married a wife, and therefore I cannot come.' Therefore, that servant came back and told his lord about these excuses.**

142. **Then the master of the house became angry and said to his servant, 'Go out quickly into the streets and lanes of the city, and bring the poor, and the maimed, and the halt, and the blind. And the servant said, 'Lord, it is done as you have commanded, and yet there is still more room.' And the lord said to the servant, 'Go out into the**

highways and hedges, and compel others to come in, so that my house may be filled. For I say to you, that none of those men who were first invited will taste of my supper."

143. And Jesus turned, and said to them, "If any *man* comes to me, and does not hate his father, and mother, and wife, and children, and brethren, and sisters, thus, and his own life also, he cannot be my disciple. And whoever does not bear his cross, and come after me, cannot be my disciple. For which of you, intending to build a tower, does not sit down first, and count the cost, to see if he has enough funds to finish it. Unless, unhappily, after he has laid the foundation he is not able to finish *it,* all who see it will mock him, Saying, This man began to build this tower, and was not able to finish it. Similarly, what king, going to make war against another king, does not first sits down and consult whether he is able with ten thousand men be able to meet him who comes against him with twenty thousand? Or else, while the other is yet a great way off, he sends an ambassador, and offers conditions of peace. So likewise, whichever of you that does not forsake all that he has cannot be my disciple."

144. "Salt *is* good: but if the salt has lost its flavor, how can it be used as seasoning? It is fit neither for the land, or even for the dunghill, an*d* men will cast it out. He that has ears to hear, let him hear this!"

145. Then the publicans and sinners drew near to hear him. And the Pharisees and scribes murmured among themselves, saying, 'This man receives sinners, and eats with them'.

146. And he spoke this parable to them, saying, **"Which of you,** having an hundred sheep, if he loses one of them, does not leave the ninety and nine in the wilderness, and go after the one that is lost, until he finds it? And when he has found *it,* he lays *it* on his shoulders, rejoicing. And when he comes home, he calls together *his* friends and neighbors, saying to them, 'Rejoice with me; for I have found my sheep which was lost.' I say to you, that the same joy will be found in heaven over one sinner who repents, more than over ninety and nine just persons, who need no repentance.

147. Also, what woman having ten pieces of silver, if she lose one piece, does not light a candle, and sweep the house, and seek it out diligently until she finds *it?* And when she has found *it,* she calls *her* friends and *her* neighbors together, saying, 'Rejoice with me; for I have found the piece that I had lost.' Likewise, I say to you, there is joy in the presence of the angels of God over one sinner that repents.

148. And he then said, 'A certain man had two sons: And the younger of them said to *his* father, Father, give me the portion of goods that belongs *to me.* And he divided *their inheritance out to them.* And not many days afterward, the younger son gathered all his stuff together, and took a journey into a far country, and there wasted his substance with riotous living. And when he had spent everything, there arose a mighty famine in that land; and he began to be in need. And he went and hired himself out to a citizen of that country, who sent him into the fields to feed his swine. And he gladly filled his belly with the husks that the swine ate: and no man gave him help.

149. And when he came to himself, he said, 'How many hired servants of my father's have bread enough to spare, and I perish with hunger?' I will arise and go to my father, and I will say to him, 'Father, I have sinned against heaven, and before you, I am not asking to be called your son any more, make me one of your hired servants'. Then he arose, and returned to his father.

150. However, when he was yet a great way off, his father saw him, and had compassion on him and ran and fell on his neck, and kissed him. And the son said to him, 'Father, I have sinned against heaven, and in your sight, and am no longer worrying about being called your son'. But the father said to his servants, 'Bring forth the best robe, and put *it* on him. Put a ring on his hand, and shoes on *his* feet Bring forth the fatted calf, and kill *it;* and let us eat, and be merry: For this is my son who I thought was dead, and he is alive again; he was lost, and is found.' And they began to be merry.

151. Now his elder son was in the field: and as he came and drew near to the house, he heard music and dancing. And he called one of the servants, and asked what these things meant. And he was told, 'Your brother has come home; and your father has killed the fatted calf, because he has returned safe and sound.' And the elder son was angry, and would not go in. Therefore, his father came out, and sought to calm him. And he complained to *his* father, Lo, for these many years I have served you, not at any time have I transgressed your commandments and

yet you never even gave me a goat, so that I might make merry with my friends.

152. But as soon as your other son came back who has devoured your living with harlots, you have killed the fatted calf for him. And the father said to him, 'Son, you are ever with me, and all that I have is yours. It was right that we should make merry, and be glad: for this is your brother who we thought was dead, and he is alive again; and who was lost, and now has been found."

153. And Jesus continued speaking to his disciples, "**There was a certain rich man, who had a steward, who was accused of wasting his goods. And he called him, and said to him, 'What is it that I hear about you? Give an account of your stewardship; for you might not be able to be my steward any longer."**

154. Then the steward said within himself, 'What will I do? If my lord takes the stewardship away from me: I cannot dig; I am ashamed to beg.' I am resolved, that, if I am put out of the stewardship, maybe the other landlords might hire me into their houses. Therefore, he called every one of his lord's debtors *to him,* and said to the first, 'How much do you owe to my lord?' And he said, 'A hundred measures of oil'. And he said to him, 'Take your bill, and sit down quickly, and write fifty'. Then said he to another, how much do you owe? And he said, 'A hundred measures of wheat.' And he said to him,' Take out your bill, and write eighty.'

155. And that last lord complimented the unjust steward, because he thought he had done wisely: for the children

of the world are in their generation wiser than the children of righteousness.

156. And I say to you, if you make yourselves friends of the mammon of unrighteousness, Prepare! So that, when you fail, they may receive you into their everlasting tribulations.

157. He that is faithful in that which is least, is faithful also in that which is great: and he that is unjust with the least of things is also unjust with that which is great. If you have not been faithful to the unrighteous mammon, who will commit to your trust, true riches? And if you have not been faithful with that which is another man's, who will give you something that is your own?

158. No servant can serve two masters: for either he will hate the one, and love the other; or else he will hold to the one, and despise the other. You cannot serve God and mammon!"

159. And the Pharisees, who were covetous, heard all these things: and they derided him. And Jesus said to them, "**You are men who justify yourselves before men; but God knows your hearts: for that which is highly esteemed among men is an abomination in the sight of God. The law and the prophets** *ruled* **until John: since that time, the kingdom of God is what is preached, and every man is pressed into it. It is easier for heaven and earth to pass, than for one title of this law to fail. Whoever puts away his wife, and marries another commits adultery: and whoever marries her that is divorced from** *her* **husband commits adultery also.**

160. There was a certain rich man, who was clothed in purple and fine linen, and fared sumptuously every day: And there was a certain beggar named Lazarus, who laid at his gate, full of sores, And desiring to be fed with the crumbs which fell from the rich man's table, even the dogs came and licked his sores.

161. And it came to pass, that the beggar died, and was carried by the angels into Abraham's bosom: the rich man died, and was buried. In Hell, he lifted up his eyes, being in torment, and saw Abraham afar off, and Lazarus in his bosom. And he cried and said, 'Father Abraham, have mercy on me, and send Lazarus so that he may dip the tip of his finger in water, and cool my tongue; for I am tormented in this flame.'

162. However, Abraham said, 'Son, remember that you in your lifetime received many good things, and likewise Lazarus evil things: but now he is comforted, and you are tormented.'

163. 'And beside all this, between us and you there is a great gulf is fixed so that they who would pass from here to you cannot. Nor can those come to us, who are there with you.' Then Lazarus said, 'Therefore, I pray to you, Father, that you would send him to my father's house: For I have five brothers, so that he may testify to them, unless they also end up in this place of torment.' Abraham said to him, 'They have Moses and the prophets; let them hear them.'

164. And he said, 'No, father Abraham: but if one went to them from the dead, they will repent.' And he said to him, 'If they cannot hear Moses and the prophets, they

will not be persuaded, even though someone rose from the dead.'"

165. Then Jesus said to the disciples, **"It is impossible that offences will not come: but woe *unto him,* through whom they come! It would be better for him that a millstone were hanged about his neck, and he cast into the sea, than that he should offend one of these little ones.**

166. **Take heed to yourselves: If your brother trespasses against you, rebuke him; and if he repents, forgive him. And if he trespasses against you seven times in a day, and seven times in a day turn again to you, saying, I repent; you must forgive him."**

167. And the apostles said to the 'Master, Increase our faith'. And the Jesus said, **"If you had faith as a grain of mustard seed, you might say to this sycamore tree, 'Be plucked up by the root, and be planted in the sea;' it would obey you. But which of you, having a servant plowing or feeding cattle, will say to him by and by, when he has come from the field, 'Go and sit down and eat?' rather than say to him, 'Make ready so that I may eat, gird yourself, and serve me, until I have eaten and drank. Then afterward you can eat and drink'. Does he thank that servant because he did the things that were commanded him? I think not. So likewise for you, when you have done well all those things that are commanded, will you say, 'We are good servants, we have done well that which was our duty to do?' I think not."**

168. **And it came to pass, as he went to Jerusalem, that he passed through the midst of Samaria and Galilee. And as he entered into a certain village, ten men met him there

who were lepers, who stood afar off: And they lifted up *their* voices, and said, 'Jesus, Master, have mercy on us'. And when he saw *them,* he said to them**, "Go show yourselves to the priests. And it came to pass that, as they left, they were cleansed."**

169. And one of them, when he saw that he was healed, turned back, and with a loud voice glorified God and fell down on *his* face at Jesus' feet, giving him thanks: even though he was a Samaritan. And Jesus responded and said, **"Were there not ten cleansed? Where *are* the other nine? Of those that that were healed cannot one be found to give glory to God, except this stranger?"** And he said to him who returned, **"Arise, go your way: your faith has made you whole."**

170. And when the Pharisees demanded of him when the kingdom of God should come, he answered them and said, **"The kingdom of God does not come with observation: Neither will they say, Lo here! Or, lo there! For, behold, the kingdom of God is within you.** And he said to his disciples, **"The days will come, when you will desire to see more days with the Son of Man, and you will not see *it.* And they will say to you, See here; or, see there: Do not go after them, or follow them For as the lightning, that lightens out of the one part under heaven and shines into the other part under heaven; so will also the Son of man be in his day.**

171. **First he must suffer many things, and be rejected by this generation. And as it was in the days of Noah, so will it be in the days of the Son of man. They ate, they drank, they married wives, they were given in marriage, until the day**

that Noah entered into the ark, and the flood came, and destroyed them all.

172. it was Likewise also as in the days of Lot; they ate, they drank, they bought, they sold, they planted, they built; But the same day that Lot went out of Sodom it rained fire and brimstone from heaven, and destroyed *them* all. Even thus will it be in the day when the Son of man will be revealed. In that day, he who will be upon the housetop, and his stuff in the house, let him not come down to take it away: and he that is in the field, let him likewise not return back. Remember Lot's wife.

173. **Whoever will seek to save his life will lose it; and whoever will lose his life will preserve it. I tell you, in that night there will be two *men* in one bed, the one will be taken, and the other will be left. Two *women* will be grinding together; the one will be taken, and the other left. Two *men* will be in the field; the one will be taken, and the other left."** And they implored him, 'Taken where, Lord'? And he said to them, **"Wherever the body is, there will the vultures be gathered together."**

174. And he spoke a parable to them *to this end,* that men ought always to pray, and not faint of heart; Saying, **"There was a judge in a city, who did not fear God, neither regarded man: And there was a widow in that city; and she came to him, saying, 'Avenge me of my adversary.' However, he would not for a while: but afterward he said within himself, 'Even though I do fear not God, nor regard man. This widow troubles me; I will avenge her, unless by her continual complaints she wearies me."** And Jesus said, "Hear what the unjust judge said. Will not God avenge his

own chosen ones, who cry day and night to him, even though he endures a long time with them? I tell you that he will avenge them speedily. Even so, when the Son of man comes, he will find little faithful here on earth?"

175. And he spoke this parable to certain men who trusted in themselves that they were righteous and despised others: "**Two men went up into the temple to pray; the one a Pharisee, and the other a publican. The Pharisee stood and prayed thus with himself, 'God, I thank you, that I am not as other men** *are,* **extortionist, unjust, adulterers, or even as this publican. I fast twice in the week; I give tithes of all that I possess.' And the publican, standing afar off, would not lift up so much as** *his* **eyes to heaven, but beat upon his breast, saying, God be merciful to me a sinner. I tell you, that this second man went home to his house justified as righteous,** *rather than* **the first man. For everyone who exalts himself will be abased; and he that humbles himself will be exalted."**

176. And people brought infants to him, that he would touch them: but when *his* disciples saw *it,* they rebuked them. But Jesus called them *to him,* and said, "**Allow the little children to come to me, and forbid them not: for of such is the kingdom of God. Verily, I say to you, Whoever will not receive the kingdom of God as a little child will in no way enter therein."**

177. And a certain ruler asked him, saying, 'Good Master, what will I do to inherit eternal life? And Jesus said to him, "**Why do you call me good? None** *are* **good, save one, and** *that is* **God. You know the commandments, Do not commit adultery, Do not kill, Do not steal, Do not bear false**

witness, Honor your father and your mother." And the man said, All these have I kept from my youth up. Now when Jesus heard these things, he said to him, "**Yet you lack one thing: sell all that you have, and distribute it to the poor, and if you want treasure in heaven: and come, follow me.**" And when he heard this, he was very sorrowful: for he was very rich. And when Jesus saw that he was very sorrowful, he said, "**How difficult it will be for those who have riches enter into the kingdom of God! For it is easier for a camel to go through a needle's eye, than for a rich man to enter into the kingdom of God.**"

178. And those who heard *it* said, 'then, who can be saved'?' And he said, "**The things which are impossible with men are possible with God.**" Then Peter said, 'Lo, we have left all, and followed you'. And he said to them, "**Verily, I say to you, There is no man that has left house, or parents, or brethren, or wife, or children, for the kingdom of God's sake, Who will not receive manifold more in this present time, and in the world to come life everlasting.**"

179. Then he took *to him* the twelve, and said to them, "**Behold, we go up to Jerusalem, and all things that are written by the prophets concerning the Son of man will be accomplished. He will be delivered to the Gentiles, and will be mocked, and spitefully entreated, and spit upon: And they will scourge *him*, and put him to death: and the third day he will rise again.**" And they understood none of these things: The meaning was hid from them, and none of them knew of the things, which were spoken.

180. And it came to pass, that as he came near to Jericho, a certain blind man sat by the way side begging: And

hearing the multitude pass by, he asked what it meant. And they told him, that Jesus of Nazareth was passing by. And he cried, saying, 'Jesus, *you* Son of David, have mercy on me'. And they who went by rebuked him, saying that he should hold his peace: but he cried so much the more, '*You* Son of David, have mercy on me'. And Jesus stood, and commanded him to be brought to him: and when he came near, he asked him, saying, "**What do you want me to do for you?**" And he said, 'Lord, that I may receive my sight'. And Jesus said to him, "**Receive your sight: your faith has saved you.**" And immediately he received his sight, and followed him, glorifying God: and all the people, when they saw *it,* they gave praise unto God.

181. As *Jesus* entered and passed through Jericho, behold, *there was* a man named Zacchaeus, who was the chief among the publicans, and he was rich. And he sought to see who Jesus was; and could not for the press, because he was little of stature. And he ran ahead, and climbed up into a sycamore tree to see him: for Jesus was supposed to come that *way*. And when Jesus came to the place, he looked up, saw him, and said to him, "**Zacchaeus, make haste, and come down; for today I must abide at your house**". And he made haste, and came down, and greeted him joyfully. And when they heard it, they all murmured, saying, that he was going to be guest of a man who is a sinner.

182. And Zacchaeus stood, and said to the Lord; 'Behold, Lord, the half of my goods I give to the poor; and if I have taken anything from any man by false accusation, I will repay *him* fourfold.' And Jesus said to him, "**This day salvation has come to this house, for so much as he also is a son of**

Abraham, Also the Son of man is come to seek and to save that which was lost". And as they heard these things, he continued and spoke a parable, because he was near to Jerusalem, and because they thought that the kingdom of God would immediately appear.

183. He said, therefore, "**A certain nobleman went into a far country to receive for himself a kingdom, and then return. And he called his ten servants, and gave them ten gold coins, and said unto them, occupy yourselves until I return. However, his citizens hated him, and sent a message to him, saying, 'We will not have this *man* to reign over us.'**

184. **And it came to pass, when he returned, that he commanded these ten servants to be called to him that he had given the money, that he might know how much every man had gained by trading. The first came, saying, 'Lord, your money has grown tenfold.' In addition, he said to him, 'Well done, you are a good servant.'** Because you have been faithful with a very little, I give you authority over ten cities. And the second one came, saying, 'Lord, your coin has gained five coins. And he said likewise, to him, 'You will have authority over five cities.' And finally the last one came, saying, 'Lord, behold, *here is* your coin, which I have kept laid up in a napkin: For I feared you, because you are an austere man: you take up what you lay not down, and reap what you did not sow.'

185. And the nobleman said to him, 'Out of your own mouth will I judge you, *you* wicked servant. You knew that I was an austere man, taking up what I laid not down, and reaping what I did not sow: Why then did you not give

my money to the bank, so that at my coming I might have been returned my own plus interest?' And he said to those that stood by, Take the coin from him, and give *it* to the one that earned ten coins." (And they said to him, Lord, he has ten coins already.)

186. **"For I say to you, That to everyone who has, it will be given; and from him that has not, even that which he has will be taken away from him. But those enemies of mine, who do not want me to reign over them, bring them here, and slay *them* before me."**

187. And when he had thus spoken, Jesus left, ascending up to Jerusalem. And it came to pass, when he came near to Bethphage and Bethany, at the mount called *the Mount* of Olives, he sent out two of his disciples, Saying, **"Go into the village over there; when you enter, you will find a colt tied up, upon whom no man ever sat: loose him, and bring *him* here. And if any man asks you, 'Why do you loose *him*'? Say this to him, 'Because the Lord has need of him'".**

188. And they that were sent went their way, and found that it was as he had said to them. And as they were untying the colt, the owners said to them, 'Why are untying the colt'? And they brought him to Jesus: and they cast their garments upon the colt, and they sat Jesus on him. And as he went, they spread their clothes in the way. And when he came near to the foot of the Mount of Olives, the whole multitude and the disciples began to rejoice and praise God with a loud voice for all the mighty works that they had seen; Saying, 'Blessed *be* the King that comes in the name of the Lord: peace in heaven, and glory in the

highest.' Some of the Pharisees from among the multitude said to him, 'Master, rebuke your disciples'. And he answered and said to them, **"I tell you that, if these should hold their peace, the stones would immediately cry out."**

189. And when he came near, he beheld the city, and wept over it, Saying, **"If you had known, even you, at least in this your day, the things *which belong* unto your peace! But now they are hidden from your eyes. For the day will come upon you, when your enemies will cast a trench about you, and encompass you around, and keep you in on every side, And will lay you even with the ground, and your children within you; and they will not leave in you one stone upon another; because you knew not the time of your visitation."**

190. And he went into the temple, and began to cast out the sellers of goods, and the buyers; Saying to them, **"It is written, my house is the house of God: but you will made it a den of thieves."** And he taught daily in the temple. However, the chief priests, the scribes, and the chief of the people sought to destroy him, but they could not find what they might do to discredit him, because all the people were very attentive to hear him.

191. And it came to pass, *that* on one of those days, as he taught the people in the temple, and preached the gospel, the chief priests and the scribes came upon him with the elders, And spoke to him, saying, 'Tell us, by what authority do you do these things? Or, who is he that gave you this authority?' And he answered and said to them, **"I will also ask you one thing; and answer me: The baptism of John, was it from heaven, or of men?"** And they reasoned within themselves, thinking, ('If we will say, From heaven; he will say, Why then did you not believe him?' However, and if we say, of men, all the people will stone us: because they are persuaded that John was a prophet.') And they answered, that they could not tell where it came from. And Jesus said to them, "**Neither will I tell you by what authority I do these things.**"

192. Then began he to speak to the people in parable; "**A certain man planted a vineyard, and let it forth to husbandmen, and went into a far country for a long time. And at the harvest season he sent a servant to the husbandmen, so that they should give him the fruit of the vineyard: but the husbandmen beat him, and sent *him* away empty. Again, he sent another servant: and they beat him also, and treated him shamefully, and sent him away empty. Again he sent a third: and they wounded him also, and cast *him* out.**

193. **Then the lord of the vineyard said, 'What will I do? I will send my beloved son: it may be they will respect *him* when they see him.' However, when the husbandmen saw him, they reasoned among themselves, saying, this is the heir: come; let us kill him, so that the inheritance may be ours. Therefore, they cast him out of the vineyard, and killed *him*.**

194. **What therefore will the lord of the vineyard do unto them?** Answering himself, Jesus said, "**He will come and destroy these husbandmen, and will give the vineyard to others**". And when the priests heard *it,* they said, 'God forbid'! And he looked at them, and said, "**What is this**

then that is written, 'The stone which the builders rejected, the same is become the cornerstone?'

195. And the chief priests and the scribes immediately sought to lay hands on him; and they feared the people: because they perceived that he had spoken this parable against them. They watched *him,* and sent forth spies, who should pretended to be honorable men, so that they might take hold of his words, so that they might deliver him to the power and authority of the governor.

196. And the spies asked him, saying, 'Master, we know that you say and teach rightly, nor do you have fear of any person, but teach the way of God truly. Is it lawful for us to give tribute unto Caesar, or not?' However, he perceived their craftiness, and said to them, **"Why do you tempt me? Show me a penny. Whose image and engraving is on it?"** They answered and said, 'Caesar's.' In addition, he said to them, **"Render therefore unto Caesar the things which be Caesar's, and unto God the things which be God's."** However, they could not take hold of his words before the people: and they marveled at his answer, and held their peace.

197. Then certain of the Sadducees came to *him,* who deny that there is any resurrection; and they asked him, Saying, 'Master, Moses wrote for us, If any man's brother die, having a wife, and he die without children, that his brother should take his wife, and raise up seed unto his brother. There were therefore seven brothers: and the first took a wife, and died without children. And the second took her to wife, and he died childless. And the third took her; and in like manner the seven also, and they left no children,

and died. Last of all the woman died also. Therefore, in the resurrection whose wife is she? For seven had her to wife.'

198. And Jesus responded to them, "**The children of this world marry, and are given in marriage: But they who will be accounted as concerned about obtaining that world, and the resurrection from the dead, neither marry, nor are given in marriage. Neither can they die any more: for they are equal to the angels; and are the children of God, being the children of the resurrection. Now that the dead are raised, even Moses showed at the bush when he called the Lord the God of Abraham, and the God of Isaac, and the God of Jacob. For he is not a God of the dead, but of the living: for all live because of him.**"

199. Then certain of the scribes answered said, 'Master, you have said well'. And after that, they dared not ask him any *question at all.* And he said to them, "**How can they say that Christ is David's son? And David himself said in the book of Psalms, the LORD said to my Lord, Sit on my right hand until I make your enemies your footstool. David therefore calls him Lord, how is he then his son?**"

200. Then, within the hearing of all the people, he said to his disciples, "**Beware of the scribes, who desire to walk in long robes, and love greetings in the markets, and the highest seats in the synagogues, and the chief rooms at feasts; Who devour widows' houses, and for a show make long speeches: the same will receive greater damnation.**"

201. And he looked up, and saw the rich men casting their gifts into the treasury. And he saw a certain poor widow casting in two pennies. And he said, "**Truly, I say to you, that this**

poor widow has cast in more than they all: For all these have cast in but part their riches in offerings to God: but she in her poverty has cast in all the living that she had."

202. And as some spoke of the temple, how it was adorned with goodly stones and gifts, he said, **"As for these things which you behold, the days will come, in the which there will not be left one stone upon another, that will not be thrown down."** And they asked him, saying, 'Master, but when will these things happen? And what sign will there be when these things come to pass?'

203. And he said, **"Take heed that you are not deceived: for many will come in my name, saying, I am *Christ;* and the time draws near: therefore do not go after them. When you will hear of wars and commotions, do not be terrified: for these things must first come to pass; but the end *is* not uncertain."** Then said he to them, **"Nation will rise against nation, and kingdom against kingdom: And great earthquakes will happen in diverse places, and famines, and pestilences; and fearful sights and great signs will be sent from heaven.**

204. However, before all these things happen, they will lay their hands on you, and persecute you, delivering you up to the synagogues, and into prisons, and bring you before kings and rulers for my name's sake. And they will turn to you for testimony. Settle *it* therefore in your hearts, not to meditate before you answer: For I will give you a voice and wisdom, which none your adversaries will be able to answer or resist. In addition, you will be betrayed both by parents, and brethren, and kinsfolk, and friends; and *some* of you will they cause to be put to death.

205. And you will be hated by all *men* for my name's sake. However, not a hair of your head will perish. With patience, possess you your souls. And when you will see Jerusalem en compassed by armies, then you will know that the desolation thereof is near. Then let them who are in Judaea flee to the mountains; and let them who are in the midst of it depart out; and let not them that are in the country return there.

206. For these are the days of vengeance, that all things which are written may be fulfilled. But woe unto them who are with child, and to them that give suck in those days! For there will be great distress in the land, and wrath upon this people. And they will fall by the edge of the sword, and will be led away captive into all nations: and Jerusalem will be trodden down by the Gentiles, until the times of the Gentiles are fulfilled.

207. And there will be signs in the sun, and in the moon, and in the stars; and upon the earth, distress, and perplexity of nations; the sea and the waves roaring; Men's hearts failing them for fear, and from looking after those things which are coming on the earth: for the powers of heaven will be shaken. Then will they see the Son of man coming in a cloud with power and great glory. And when these things begin to come to pass, then look up, and lift up your heads; for your redemption draws near."

208. And he spoke to them a parable; "**Behold the fig tree, and all the trees; when they now shoot forth, you see and know of your own selves that summer is now near at hand. So likewise, you, when you see these things come to pass, know you that the kingdom of God is near at

hand. Verily, I say to you, this generation will not pass away, until all is fulfilled. Heaven and earth will pass away: but my words will not pass away.

209. **And take heed to yourselves, lest at any time your hearts be overcharged with excess, and drunkenness, and cares of this life, so that day might come upon you unaware. For as a snare will it come on all them that dwell on the face of the whole earth. Therefore, watch out and pray always, so that you may be counted as concerned about escape from all these things that will come to pass, and stand before the Son of man."**

210. In the daytime, he was teaching in the temple; and at night, he went out, and stayed at the hill that is called *the Mount* of Olives. And all the people came early in the morning to the temple to hear him.

211. Now, the feast of unleavened bread drew near, which is called the Passover. And the chief priests and scribes contemplated how they might kill him, for they feared the people.

212. Then came the day of unleavened bread, when the Passover must be celebrated. And he sent Peter and John, saying, **"Go and prepare us a place for the Passover, so that we may eat"**. And they said to him, 'Where do you wish that we should go to prepare'? And he said to them, **"Behold, when you enter into the city, you will meet a man bearing a pitcher of water; follow him to the house where he enters. And you will say to the good man of the house, 'The Master asks of you', 'Where is the guest chamber, where I will eat the Passover with my**

disciples'? And he will show you a large upper room furnished: make ready there."

213. And they went, and they found it as Jesus had told them, and they made ready the Passover. And when the hour came, he sat down, and the twelve apostles with him. And he said to them, **"With longing, I have desired to eat this Passover with you before I suffer: For I say to you, I will not eat any more thereof, until it be fulfilled in the kingdom of God."** And he took the cup, and gave thanks, and said, **"Take this, and divide *it* among yourselves: For I say unto you, I will not drink of the fruit of the vine, until the kingdom of God will come."**

214. And he took bread, and gave thanks, and broke it, and gave it to them, saying, **"This is my body which is given for you: do this in remembrance of me."** Likewise with the cup after supper, saying, **"This cup is the new testament of my blood, which is shed for you.**

215. **But, behold, the hand of him that betrayed me *is* with me on the table. And truly the Son of man goes as his destiny has been determined: but woe to that man by whom he is betrayed!"** And they began to enquire among themselves, which of them it was that should do this awful thing.

216. And there was strife among them, as to which of them would be accounted the greatest. And he said to them, **"The kings of the Gentiles exercise lordship over them, and they that exercise authority upon them are called benefactors. However, for you it will not be so: but he that is greatest among you, let him be as the younger; and he that is chief, let him be as he who serves.**

217. **For whether he *is* greater, that sits at meat, or he that serves? *Is* it not he that sits at meat? But I am among you as he that serves. You are they who will continue with me in my temptations. And I appoint unto you a kingdom, as my Father has appointed unto me. So That you may eat and drink at my table in my kingdom, and sit on thrones judging the twelve tribes of Israel."**

218. And Jesus said, **"Simon, Simon, behold, Satan has desired *to have* you, that he may sift *you* as wheat: But I have prayed for you, that your faith should not fail: and when you are converted, strengthen your brothers."** And Simon Peter said to him, 'Lord, I am ready to go with you, both into prison, and to death'. And Jesus said, **"I tell you, Peter, the cock will not crow this day, before you will thrice deny that you know me. And he said unto them, when I sent you without purse, and script, and shoes, did you lack anything?"** And they said, 'No, nothing'.

219. Then he said to them, **"But now, he that has a purse, let him take *it,* and likewise *his* script: and he that has no sword, let him sell his garment, and buy one. For I say unto you, that what is written must thus be accomplished in me."** And Peter was reckoned among the transgressors: **"For the things concerning me will an end."** And they said, 'Lord, behold, here *are* two swords.' And he said to them, **"It is through."**

220. And he came out, and went, as he was accustomed, to the Mount of Olives; and his disciples followed him. And when he was at that place, he said to them, **"Pray that you enter not into temptation"**. And he withdrew from them about a stone's cast, and kneeled down, and prayed, Saying,

"Father, if you are willing, remove this cup from me." Then, "Nevertheless it is not my will, but yours, to be done."

221. And there appeared an angel to him from heaven, strengthening him. And being in an agony he prayed more earnestly: and his sweat was as if there were great drops of blood falling down to the ground. And when he rose up from prayer, and came to his disciples, he found them sleeping for sorrow, and he said to them, **"Why do you sleep? Rise and pray, unless you enter into temptation."**

222. And while he thus spoke, behold a multitude came, and he who was called Judas, one of the twelve, went before them, and drew near to Jesus to kiss him. But Jesus said to him, **"Judas, do you betray the Son of man with a kiss?"** When they who were about him saw what would follow, they said to him, 'Lord, will we smite him with the sword'?

223. And one of them hit the servant of the high priest, and cut off his right ear. And Jesus answered and said, **"You have suffered enough!"** And he touched his ear, and healed him. Then Jesus said to the chief priests, and captains of the temple, and the elders, who came up to him, **"Why do you come out as against a thief, with swords and staves? When I was with you daily in the temple, you stretched forth no hands against me: but this is your hour, and the powers of darkness."**

224. Then they took him, and led *him,* and brought him into the high priest's house. And Peter followed afar off. And when they had kindled a fire in the midst of the hall, and sat down together, Peter sat down among them. However, a certain girl beheld him as he sat by the fire, and earnestly

looked upon him, and said, this man was also with him. And he denied him, saying, 'Woman, I don't know that man!'

225. And after a little while, another person saw him, and said, 'You were also one of them'! And Peter said, 'Man, I am not'! And, in about the space of one hour, another confidently affirmed the others, saying, 'Truly, this *fellow* also was with him: for he is a Galilean.' And Peter said, 'Man, I don't know what you're talking about'! And immediately, while he spoke, the cock crowed.

226. And Peter remembered the words of the Jesus, how he had said to him, "**Before the cock crows, you will deny me three times.**" And Peter went out, and wept bitterly.

227. And the men that held Jesus mocked him, and hit *him.* Then they had blindfolded him and struck him on the face, and asked him, saying, 'Prophet! Tell us, who is it that hit you'? And they spoke many other blasphemous things against him.

228. And as soon as it was day, the elders of the people and the chief priests and the scribes came together, and led him into their council, saying, 'Are you the Christ? Tell us!' And he said to them, "**If I tell you, you will not believe: And if I also ask *you,* you will not answer me, nor will you let *me* go. Hereafter will the Son of man sit on the right hand of the power of God.**" Then they all said, 'Are you then the Son of God?' And he said to them, "**You say that I am.**" And they said, 'Why do we need any further testimony? For we ourselves have heard from his own mouth.'

229. Then whole multitude of them arose, and led him to Pilate. And they began to accuse him, saying, 'We found this

fellow perverting the nation, and forbidding people to give tribute to Caesar, saying that he himself is Christ the King.' And Pilate asked him, saying, 'Are you the King of the Jews'? And he answered him and said, **"You say it"**

230. Then Pilate said to the chief priests and *to* the people, I find no fault in this man. And they responded more fiercely, saying, 'He stirs up the people, teaching throughout all Jewry, beginning from Galilee to this place'. When Pilate heard of Galilee, he asked whether the man were a Galilean. As soon as he knew that he belonged in Herod's jurisdiction, he sent him to Herod, who was also in Jerusalem at that time.

231. And when Herod saw Jesus, he was exceeding glad: for he had desired to see him for a long *time,* because he had heard many things of him; and he hoped to see some miracle performed by him. Then he questioned him with many words; but Jesus answered him nothing. And the chief priests and scribes stood and vehemently accused him. And Herod with his men of war threatened and mocked *him,* and then dressed him in a gorgeous robe, and sent him back again to Pilate.

232. And that same day Pilate and Herod made friends with each other: because before this time there were bad feelings between them.

233. And a great company of men followed him, and women too, who also bewailed and lamented him. However, Jesus turned to them and said, **"Daughters of Jerusalem, weep not for me, but weep for yourselves, and for your children. For, behold, the days are coming, in the which they will say, Blessed *are* the barren, and the wombs that**

never bore child, and the nipples which never gave suck. Then will they begin to say to the mountains, fall on us; and to the hills, and Cover us. For if they do these things to a fertile tree, what will be done to the dry?"

234. In addition, there were two others, malefactors, who were led with him to be put to death. And when they came to the place, which is called Calvary, they crucified him there with the malefactors, one on the right hand and the other on the left.

235. Then Jesus said, "**Father, forgive them; for they know not what they do.**" And they paraded his robe, and cast lots. And the people stood watching. And the rulers with them derided *him,* saying, 'He saved others; let him save himself, if he is the Christ, the chosen of God'. And the soldiers mocked him coming to him, and offering him vinegar. And saying, 'If you are the king of the Jews, save yourself'. And a superscription was written over him in letters of Greek, and Latin, and Hebrew, 'THIS IS THE KING OF THE JEWS.' (INRI, in Roman script)

236. And one of the condemned men who was crucified with him mocked him, saying, 'If you are Christ, save yourself and us.' However, the other man answered, rebuking him, saying, 'Don't you fear God, seeing that you are in the same condemnation? And we are condemned, indeed, justly; for we receive the due reward of our deeds: but this man has done nothing wrong.' And he said to Jesus, 'Lord, remember me when you come into your kingdom' Jesus said to him, "**Verily I say to you, will you be with me today in Paradise**".

237. At the sixth hour there was a darkness over all the earth until the ninth hour. Moreover, the sun darkened, and the veil of the temple was torn in two.
238. And when Jesus had cried with a loud voice, he said, "**Father, into your hands I commend my spirit**": and having said thus, he gave up the ghost.
239. Now when the centurion saw that it was done, he glorified God, saying, 'Surely, this was a righteous man'. And all the people that came together to that sight, beholding the things, which were done, hit their breasts, and returned home. And all his acquaintances, and the women that followed him from Galilee, stood far off, beholding these things.

Arianism

From Wikipedia, the free encyclopedia

This article is about various theological concepts associated with Arius.

Not to be confused with "Aryanism" which formed the core of Nazi racial ideology.

Arianism is the theological teaching of Arius (ca. AD 250–336), a Christian presbyter from Alexandria, Egypt, concerning the relationship of the entities of the Trinity ('God the Father', 'God the Son' and 'God the Holy Spirit') and the precise nature of the Son of God. Deemed a heretic by the First Council of Nicaea of 325, Arius was later exonerated in 335 at the First Synod of Tyre, and then pronounced a heretic again after his death at the First Council of Constantinople of 381. The Roman Emperors Constantius II(337-361) and Valens (364-378) were Arians or Semi-Arians.

Arianism is defined as those teachings attributed to Arius which are in opposition to mainstream Trinitarian Christological dogma, as determined by the first two Ecumenical Councils and currently maintained by the Roman Catholic Church, the Eastern Orthodox Churches and most Protestant Churches. "Arianism" is also often used to refer to other nontrinitarian theological systems of the 4th century, which regarded Jesus Christ—the Son of God, the Logos—as either a created being (as in Arianism proper andAnomoeanism), or as neither uncreated nor created in the sense other beings are created (as in Semi-Arianism).

Origin

Main article: <u>Arian controversy</u>

Arius posed the question: "Is Jesus unbegotten?" In answer, he taught that God the Father and the Son did not exist together eternally. Further, Arius taught that the pre-incarnate Jesus was a divine being created by (and therefore inferior to) God the Father at some point, before which the Son did not exist. In English-language works, it is sometimes said that Arians believe that Jesus is or was a "creature"; in the sense of "created being". That doctrine that Arius wrote was based on Scriptures such as John 14:28 where Jesus says that the father is "greater than I", to John 17:20-26, where Jesus asks that the Apostles become "one as we are one" so that all of them, including Jesus, and God become one. This is interpreted as indicating that the oneness refers to a unity of divine thought and will, and not a unity in a co-eternal Trinity. Of all the various disagreements within the Christian Church, the Arian controversy has held the greatest force and power of theological and political conflict, with the possible exception of the Protestant Reformation. The conflict between Arianism and Trinitarian beliefs was the first major doctrinal confrontation in the Church after the legalization of Christianity by the Roman Emperor Constantine I.

The controversy over Arianism began to rise in the late 3rd century and extended over the greater part of the 4th century and involved most church members, simple believers, priests and monks as well as bishops, emperors and members of Rome's imperial family.

Yet, such a deep controversy within the Church could not have materialized in the 3rd and 4th centuries without some significant historical influences providing the basis for the Arian doctrines. Most orthodox or mainstream Christian historians define and minimize the Arian conflict as the exclusive construct of Arius and a handful of rogue bishops engaging in heresy. Of the roughly three hundred bishops in attendance at the Council of Nicea, only three bishops did not sign the Nicene Creed. However, to minimize the extent of Arianism ignores the fact that extremely prominent Emperors such as Constantius II, and Valens were Arians, as well as prominent Gothic, Vandal, and Lombard warlords both before and after the fall of the Western Roman Empire, and that none of these groups was out of the mainstream of the Roman Empire in the 4th century. After the dispute over Arius politicized the debate and a catholic or general solution to the debate was sought, with a great majority holding to the Trinitarian position, the Arian position was declared officially to be heterodox. Lucian of Antioch had contended for a christology very similar to what would later be known as Arianism and is thought to have contributed much to its development. Arius was a student of Lucian's private academy in Antioch. The Ebionites, among other early Christian groups, may also have maintained similar doctrines that can be associated with formal Lucian and Arian Christology.

While Arianism continued to dominate for several decades even within the family of the Emperor, the Imperial nobility, and higher-ranking clergy, in the end it was Trinitarianism which prevailed in the

Roman Empire at the end of the 4th century. Arianism, which had been taught by the Arian missionary Ulfilas to the Germanic tribes, was dominant for some centuries among several Germanic tribes in western Europe, especially Goths and Lombards (and significantly for the late Empire, the Vandals), but ceased to be the mainstream belief by the 8th century. Trinitarianism remained the dominant doctrine in all major branches of the Eastern and Western Church and later within Protestantism, although there have been several anti-Trinitarian movements, some of which acknowledge various similarities to classical Arianism.

Beliefs

Because most extant written material on Arianism was written by its opponents, the nature of Arian teachings is difficult to define precisely today. The letter of Auxentius, a 4th-century Arian bishop of Milan, regarding the missionary Ulfilas, gives the clearest picture of Arian beliefs on the nature of the Trinity: God the Father ("unbegotten"), always existing, was separate from the lesser Jesus Christ ("only-begotten"), born before time began and creator of the world. The Father, working through the Son, created the Holy Spirit, who was subservient to the Son as the Son was to the Father. The Father was seen as "the only true God". 1 Corinthians 8:5-6 was cited as proof text:

Indeed, even though there may be so-called gods in heaven or on earth — as in fact there are many gods and many lords — yet for us there is one God (Gk. *theos* - θεος), the Father, from whom are all things and for whom we exist, and one Lord (*kyrios* - κυριος), Jesus Christ, through whom are all things and through whom we exist.

A letter from Arius to the Arian Eusebius of Nicomedia succinctly states the core beliefs of the Arians:

Some of them say that the Son is an eructation, others that he is a production, others that he is also unbegotten. These are impieties to which we cannot listen, even though the heretics threaten us with a thousand deaths. But we say and believe and have taught, and do teach, that the Son is not unbegotten, nor in any way part of the unbegotten; and that he does not derive his subsistence from any matter; but that by his own will and counsel he has subsisted before time and before ages as perfect God, only begotten and unchangeable, and that before he was begotten, or created, or purposed, or established, he was not. For he was not unbegotten. We are persecuted, because we say that the Son has a beginning, but that God is without beginning.
—Peters , *Heresy and Authority in Medieval Europe*, p. 41

First Council of Nicaea and its aftermath

In 321, Arius was denounced by a synod at Alexandria for teaching a heterodox view of the relationship of Jesus to God the Father. Because Arius and his followers had great influence in the schools of Alexandria—counterparts to modern universities or seminaries—their theological views spread, especially in the eastern Mediterranean.

By 325, the controversy had become significant enough that the Emperor Constantine called an assembly of bishops, the First

Council of Nicaea, which condemned Arius' doctrine and formulated the Original Nicene Creed[5], forms of which are still recited in Catholic, Orthodox, Anglican, and some Protestant services. The Nicene Creed's central term, used to describe the relationship between the Father and the Son, is Homoousios, or Consubstantiality, meaning "of the same substance" or "of one being". (The Athanasian Creed is less often used but is a more overtly anti-Arian statement on the Trinity.)

The focus of the Council of Nicaea was the divinity of Christ (see Paul of Samosata and the Synods of Antioch). Arius taught that Jesus Christ was divine and was sent to earth for the salvation of mankind but that Jesus Christ was not equal to the Father (infinite, primordial origin) and to the Holy Spirit (giver of life). Under Arianism, Christ was instead notconsubstantial with God the Father since both the Father and the Son under Arius were made of "like" essence or being (see homoiousia) but not of the same essence or being (see homoousia). Ousia is essence or being, in Eastern Christianity, and is the aspect of God that is completely incomprehensible to mankind and human perception. It is all that subsists by itself and which has not its being in another. God the Father and God the Son and God the Holy Spirit all being uncreated. According to the teaching of Arius, the preexistent Logos and thus the incarnate Jesus Christ was a created being; that only the Son was directly created and begotten by God the Father, before ages, but was of a distinct, though similar, essence or substance to the Creator; his opponents argued that this would make Jesus less than God, and that this was heretical. Much of the distinction between the differing factions was over the phrasing that Christ expressed in the New Testament to express submission to God the Father. The theological term for this submission is kenosis. This Ecumenical council declared that Jesus Christ was a distinct being of God in existence or reality (hypostasis), which the Latin fathers translated as persona. Jesus was God in essence, being and or nature (ousia), which the Latin fathers translated as substantia.

Constantine is believed to have exiled those who refused to accept the Nicean creed—Arius himself, the deaconEuzoios, and the Libyan bishops Theonas of Marmarica and Secundus of Ptolemais— and also the bishops who signed the creed but refused to join in condemnation of Arius, Eusebius of Nicomedia and Theognis of Nicaea. The Emperor also ordered all copies of the *Thalia*, the book in which Arius had expressed his teachings, to beburned. However, there is no evidence that his son and ultimate successor, Constantius II, who was an Arian Christian, was exiled.

Although he was committed to maintaining what the church had defined at Nicaea, Constantine was also bent on pacifying the situation and eventually became more lenient toward those condemned and exiled at the council. First he allowed Eusebius of Nicomedia, who was a protégé of his sister, and Theognis to return once they had signed an ambiguous statement of faith. The two, and other friends of Arius, worked for Arius' rehabilitation. At the First

Synod of Tyre in AD 335, they brought accusations against Athanasius, bishop of Alexandria, the primary opponent of Arius; after this, Constantine had Athanasius banished, since he considered him an impediment to reconciliation. In the same year, the Synod of Jerusalem under Constantine's direction readmitted Arius to communion in AD 336. Arius, however, died on the way to this event in Constantinople. This was the same day Arius' own bishop prayed that if his heresy was to be propagated, the Lord take him in death that night- or better, Arius. Some scholars also suggest that Arius may have been poisoned by his opponents. Eusebius and Theognis remained in the Emperor's favour, and when Constantine, who had been a catechumen much of his adult life, accepted baptism on his deathbed, it was from Eusebius of Nicomedia.

Theological debates

The Council of Nicaea did not end the controversy, as many bishops of the Eastern provinces disputed the *homoousios*, the central term of the Nicene creed, as it had been used by Paul of Samosata, who had advocated a monarchianist Christology. Both the man and his teaching, including the term *homoousios*, had been condemned by the Synods of Antioch in 269.

Hence, after Constantine's death in 337, open dispute resumed again. Constantine's son Constantius II, who had become Emperor of the eastern part of the Empire, actually encouraged the Arians and set out to reverse the Nicene creed. His advisor in these affairs was Eusebius of Nicomedia, who had already at the Council of Nicea been the head of the Arian party, who also was made bishop of Constantinople.

Constantius used his power to exile bishops adhering to the Nicene creed, especially Athanasius of Alexandria, who fled to Rome. In 355 Constantius became the sole Emperor and extended his pro-Arian policy toward the western provinces, frequently using force to push through his creed, even exiling <u>Pope Liberius</u> and installing <u>Antipope Felix II</u>.

As debates raged in an attempt to come up with a new formula, three camps evolved among the opponents of the Nicene creed. The first group mainly opposed the Nicene terminology and preferred the term *homoiousios* (alike in substance) to the Nicene *homoousios*, while they rejected Arius and his teaching and accepted the equality and coeternality of the persons of the Trinity. Because of this centrist position, and despite their rejection of Arius, they were called "semi-Arians" by their opponents. The second group also avoided invoking the name of Arius, but in large part followed Arius' teachings and, in another attempted compromise wording, described the Son as being like (*homoios*) the Father. A third group explicitly called upon Arius and described the Son as unlike (*anhomoios*) the Father. Constantius wavered in his support between the first and the second party, while harshly persecuting the third.

The debates between these groups resulted in numerous synods, among them the Council of Sardica in 343, the Council of Sirmium in 358 and the doubleCouncil of Rimini and Seleucia in 359, and no less than fourteen further creed formulas between 340 and 360, leading the pagan observer Ammianus Marcellinusto comment sarcastically: "The highways were covered with galloping bishops." None of these attempts was acceptable to the defenders of Nicene orthodoxy: writing about the latter councils, Saint Jerome remarked that the world "awoke with a groan to find itself Arian."

After Constantius' death in 361, his successor Julian, a devotee of Rome's pagan gods, declared that he would no longer attempt to favor one church faction over another, and allowed all exiled bishops to return; this had the objective of further increasing dissension among Christians. The Emperor Valens, however, revived Constantius' policy and supported the "Homoian" party, exiling bishops and often using force. During this persecution many bishops were exiled to the other ends of the Empire, (e.g., Hilarius of Poitiers to the Eastern provinces). These contacts and the common plight subsequently led to a rapprochement between the Western supporters of the Nicene creed and the *homoousios* and the Eastern semi-Arians.

Theodosius and the Council of Constantinople

Main article: Theodosius I

It was not until the co-reigns of Gratian and Theodosius that Arianism was effectively wiped out among the ruling class and elite of the Eastern Empire. Theodosius' wife St Flacilla was instrumental in his campaign to end Arianism. Valens died in the Battle of Adrianople in 378 and was succeeded by Theodosius I, who adhered to the Nicene creed. This allowed for settling the dispute.

Two days after Theodosius arrived in Constantinople, November 24, 380, he expelled the Homoian bishop, Demophilus of Constantinople, and surrendered the churches of that city to Gregory Nazianzus, the leader of the rather small Nicene community there, an act which provoked rioting. Theodosius had just been baptized, by bishop Acholius of Thessalonica, during a severe illness, as was common in the early Christian world. In February he and Gratian published an edict that all their subjects should profess the faith of the bishops of Rome and Alexandria (i.e., the Nicene faith), or be handed over for punishment for not doing so.

Although much of the church hierarchy in the East had opposed the Nicene creed in the decades leading up to Theodosius' accession, he managed to achieve unity on the basis of the Nicene creed. In 381, at the Second Ecumenical Council in Constantinople, a group of mainly Eastern bishops assembled and accepted the Nicene Creed of 381, which was supplemented in regard to the Holy Spirit, as well as some other changes: see Comparison between Creed of 325 and

Creed of 381. This is generally considered the end of the dispute about the Trinity and the end of Arianism among the Roman, non-Germanic peoples.

Early medieval Germanic kingdoms

Main articles: Gothic Christianity and Germanic Christianity

However, during the time of Arianism's flowering in Constantinople, the Gothic convert Ulfilas (later the subject of the letter of Auxentius cited above) was sent as a missionary to the Gothic barbarians across the Danube, a mission favored for political reasons by emperor Constantius II. Ulfilas' initial success in converting this Germanic people to an Arian form of Christianity was strengthened by later events. When the Germanic peoples entered the Roman Empire and founded successor-kingdoms in the western part, most had been Arian Christians for more than a century

The conflict in the 4th century had seen Arian and Nicene factions struggling for control of the Church. In contrast, in the Arian German kingdoms established on the wreckage of the Western Roman Empire in the 5th century, there were entirely separate Arian and Nicene Churches with parallel hierarchies, each serving different sets of believers. The Germanic elites were Arians, and the majority population was Nicene. Many scholars see the persistence of Germanic Arianism as a strategy that was followed in order to differentiate the Germanic elite from the local inhabitants and their culture and also to maintain the Germanic elite's separate group identity. Most Germanic tribes were generally tolerant of the Nicene beliefs of their subjects. However, the Vandals tried for several decades to force their Arian beliefs on their North African Nicene subjects, exiling Nicene clergy, dissolving monasteries, and exercising heavy pressure on non-conforming Christians.

By the beginning of the 8th century, these kingdoms had either been conquered by Nicene neighbors (Ostrogoths, Vandals, Burgundians) or their rulers had accepted Nicene Christianity (Visigoths, Lombards).

The Franks were unique among the Germanic peoples in that they entered the empire as pagans and converted to Nicene(Catholic) Christianity directly, guided by their king Clovis.

Remnants in the West

However, much of southeastern Europe and central Europe, including many of the Goths and Vandals respectively, had embraced Arianism (the Visigothsconverted to Arian Christianity in 376), which led to Arianism being a religious factor in various wars in the Roman Empire.[1] In the west, organized Arianism survived in North Africa, in Hispania, and parts of Italy until it was finally suppressed in the 6th and 7th centuries (in part due to the advance of Islam). Later, during the Protestant reformation, a religious sect in Poland known as the Polish Brethren were commonly referred to as Arians due to their rejection of the Trinity.

"Arian" as a polemical epithet

In many ways, the conflict around Arian beliefs in the fourth, fifth and sixth centuries helped firmly define the centrality of the Trinity in Nicene Christian theology. As the first major intra-Christian conflict after Christianity's legalization, the struggle between Nicenes and Arians left a deep impression on the institutional memory of Nicene churches.

Archbishop Dmitri of the Orthodox Church in America said Islam is the largest descendant of Arianism today. There is some superficial similarity in Islam's teaching that Jesus was a great prophet, but very distinct from God, although Islam sees Jesus as a human messenger of God without the divine properties that Arianism attributes to Christ. Islam sees itself as a continuation of the Jewish and Christian traditions and reveres many of the same prophets, though Islam denies the crucifixion and resurrection of Jesus and historical Arians claimed it.

Thus, over the past 1,500 years, some Christians have used the term *Arian* to refer to those groups that see themselves as worshiping Jesus Christ or respecting his teachings, but do not hold to the Nicene creed. Despite the frequency with which this name is used as a polemical label, there has been no historically continuous survival of Arianism into the modern era.

Other religious movements considered Arian

There have been religious movements holding beliefs that either they, or their opponents, have considered Arian. To quote the *Encyclopaedia Britannica*'s article on Arianism: "In modern times some Unitarians are virtually Arians in that they are unwilling either to reduce Christ to a mere human being or to attribute to him a divine nature identical with that of the Father."[1] However, their doctrines cannot be considered representative of traditional Arian doctrines or vice-versa.

A religious movement reputed to practice a form of Arianism (or "Semi-Arianism") are Jehovah's Witnesses.[1] They consider Jesus Christ to be divine and unlike other creatures, but not equal to the one God. And although they are not Trinitarians or Athanasians, they disagree with Arius' views in many respects. Arius, for example, denied that the Son could really know the Father while Jehovah's Witnesses believe that the Son 'fully knows' the Father, and also that the Son, as 'the Word who became flesh', is "the one that has explained him." (Mt 11:27; John 1:14, 18) They believe it is vital to come to know God. And although Arius did not accept Athanasius' theory that the holy spirit was co-equal and of the same substance as the Father, he did consider the spirit to be a person or a high angel. Jehovah's Witnesses believe the Holy Spirit is not an actual person but rather is God's divine breath or active force.

Printed in the USA
CPSIA information can be obtained
at www.ICGtesting.com
LVHW011209090624
782727LV00008B/564